DANCING
CORN DOGS
IN THE NIGHT

DANCING CORN DOGS IN THE NIGHT

REAWAKENING YOUR CREATIVE SPIRIT

DON HAHN

HYPERION

NEW YORK

Copyright © 1998 Don Hahn

Library of Congress Cataloging-in-Publication Data

Hahn, Don.
    Dancing corn dogs in the night : reawakening your creative spirit / by Don Hahn. — 1st ed.
        p.   cm.
    ISBN 0-7868-6374-9
    1. Creative ability.   2. Creative thinking.   I. Title.
BF408.H24   1999
153.3'5—dc21   98-35778
                                                         CIP

Designed by Gloria Adelson

FIRST EDITION

10 9 8 7 6 5 4 3 2 1

For Mom and Dad

ACKNOWLEDGMENTS

I'm indebted to hundreds of people at the Walt Disney Studios who have taught me about art and life—people like Walt Stanchfield who showed me how to paint with coffee and Eric Larson who took interest in my drawings when there was no reason to. People like Peter Schneider and Thomas Schumacher who supply something that no artist should ever take for granted: a safe haven for creation. And people like Patti Conklin who take care of me, which is no small thing.

The idea for this book took shape when Wendy Lefkon bought me a Caesar salad and an iced tea one sunny September day in Florida and said she wanted me to write about creativity. I am forever grateful for her support, advice, and unfailing faith in the idea that a cartoon producer could write a meaningful book on the creative spirit. And finally my greatest thanks to my family past and present: Paul, Elsie, Bertha, Randy, Margaret, Jim, Linda, Kara, Kathy, Don, Greg, Mark, and the inimitable Denise and Emilie for the blessed life we have all shared.

CONTENTS

PROLOGUE

I love my hardware store. Maybe it's a "guy thing," but I really love my hardware store. Late on Saturday morning after I've read the newspaper and drained the coffee pot, I casually find any excuse to step out and make the pilgrimage to my hardware store. It's called Virgil's.

"Be right back," I shout knowing that I won't. My wife smiles an understanding smile. I drive the few short blocks to Virgil's with the anticipation of a dog on his first car ride—eyes wide, sloppy grin, head out the window drooling occasionally. I park the car and walk in.

As I approach, the automatic doors swing open to meet me in an automated sign of welcome. There I stop and stand, smiling faintly, like a baby with gas, nut in hand looking for my perfect bolt. The others are there too. Tousled unshaven men like me, with Mona Lisa smiles, standing, staring, holding their nuts and looking for their bolts, too. It's our little secret corner of the universe.

Why? Because here is the stuff that life is made of. I can create anything here. I can walk the aisles for hours staring expectantly at endless bins of possibilities, just waiting for the right idea to jump out at me. Not only are there everyday items here like nails, switches, wire, and chain, there are enchanted items, too. Items like Velcro, superglue, and duct tape. Here I can find paint and faucets alongside bug lights and books on mulching. They even have helpers at my hardware store—mature men named Bob and Randy sporting red vests and waiting to tell me where to find plumb bobs or how to snap a chalk line. At Virgil's I can even get eggs and night crawlers while I have a key made.

It seems like I grew up here at Virgil's. I can almost see my grandpa showing me how to pick out a straight stud, and my dad teaching me the finer points of tub caulk. The possibilities seemed endless. It was a place where I could build anything, create anything, and do anything. I felt like I could rule the world from right there in aisle 6B of Virgil's.

Creativity is a little like my hardware store. I come in the door with my problem and search the wonderful, endless bins of possibilities until I find a solution. Sometimes you ask for help and sometimes the answers are unexpected, but I always leave with confidence that my small brown paper bag holds the solution.

Read this book like you would browse through your

hardware store. Look at its ideas and stories—some that may apply to you and some that may not—then take from it that little nut of an idea about creativity that can bring joy and enrichment to your life.

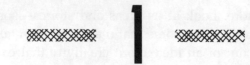

THE

Dancing Corn Dogs in the Night

It's ten o'clock at night. My parents are in the living room howling at Crazy Guggenham on *The Jackie Gleason Show*, and I've secretly smuggled a flashlight into bed. Maybe that doesn't sound like big-city excitement but at five years old, well, it was a treat. I'd sneak under the covers with a flashlight from the kitchen drawer and pajama bottoms stuffed with green plastic army men. When the lights went out, I'd flip on the flashlight and reenact the allied invasion of Normandy beneath the sheets for what seemed like hours.

When I got bored with that, I'd punch some holes in a piece of foil and put it over the flashlight, securing it with

4

a rubber band from that morning's newspaper. Suddenly my room was a planetarium full of stars and constellations. The Big Dipper was way up there next to my model monster collection and the North Star burned brightly just above my sock drawer. I once stuffed a giant colander into my pajama bottoms and smuggled it into my bedroom. With a flashlight and a colander, I could recreate the entire Milky Way galaxy on my ceiling. I didn't think my mom suspected a thing, but in retrospect, I'm sure she just shook her head and said, "There he goes again with that darned colander in his pants." Dad probably snorted a proud snort and went back to Jackie Gleason.

Sometimes I would prop the flashlight up on my bookshelf and try making silhouettes on the wall. I could do a passable barking dog, a butterfly, and a bust of Lincoln, but the big crowd pleaser was a lifelike silhouette of Richard Nixon in a birch-bark canoe, a feat that I must say was not unimpressive.

It was about the same time that I had my first run-in with the movies. My mom and dad had made some popcorn, dressed my brother and sister and me in our jammies, and loaded us into the back of our pink Rambler station wagon and we drove off to the Rosecrans Drive-in for a double bill: *One Hundred and One Dalmatians* and one of those Doug McClure movies titled *Journey to Somewhere Underground with Big Rubber Dinosaurs.*

After we'd found our perfect parking place and hung the Hi-Fidelity speaker on my dad's window, we'd eat popcorn and play Twister, waiting for the show to begin. And then it came. All the lights in the drive-in went out, the kids at the big playground underneath the screen ran back to their cars, and a beacon of light beamed through the darkness from the snack bar roof onto what appeared to be the biggest white rectangle I had ever seen. The first image that night was a quartet of animated snacks delivering a snappy jingle touting the snack bar.

I was mesmerized. Sure, I had watched television, but the difference between watching *Bonanza* on a sixteen-inch black-and-white TV screen and watching a gigantic singin' and dancin' corn dog at the drive-in was life transforming. This was better than my flashlight and colander. Much better. I became glued to the light in the darkness. There I was with my family in a station wagon parked on a hot Saturday night with two hundred other cars. There were kids, adults, horny teenagers, and pimple-faced snack bar attendants all staring at the light in the darkness (or was it pimple-faced teenagers and horny snack bar attendants? Oh well, you get the idea).

I'm not an anthropologist but it seemed to my five-year-old brain that I was experiencing a primal joy as I stared at this light in the darkness. It was probably the same joy cavemen experienced from staring at a campfire in the frigid void of night—except without the giant dancing corn dog part.

Three hours, two features, and seven cans of root beer later, I was hooked on movies and I had to go to the bathroom in a profound way. I was too young to understand the concept of a double bill, and for years I wanted to go back to see that movie again—you know, the one with Pongo, Doug McClure, and a giant corn dog. Staring at the big rectangle would be the most amazing fun I had ever had in the back of a station wagon for years to come.

Foundations

All human creativity is like a light in the darkness, and just as light is made up of three primary colors, the foundation of creative thinking is formed from three critical elements. First you need a huge amount of information. Fortunately we are alive in the middle of the biggest information boom since the invention of movable type five hundred years ago. Modern media is everywhere, and your ability to get information on the Internet is a recent phenomenon that puts nearly every man, woman, and child in contact with not only the 644,009 entries listed when you type in the words *Pamela Lee*, but also with the greatest thinkers and libraries known to man.

Secondly you need an untiring interest. You need the will and desire to play with ideas into the dead of night— to turn things over in your head and play with the problems of your craft just because that's what you love to do. You need the passion to bring loads and loads of raw material to consciousness for consideration.

And finally you must have not only the ability but the ruthlessness to take out the trash. Nobody can think of only good ideas or write only touching sensitive prose all the time. If we've done our creative task properly, first we've done our homework, next we've created tons of fodder for thought, and finally we've weeded though our thoughts, separating the rocks from the gems, always mindful that time changes things and today's junk might be tomorrow's gem.

Sadly there is no National Bureau of Taste or arbiter of good and bad ideas. That choice between good idea and bad idea is up to you. It's a very personal choice, too—as personal as the clothes you wear and the food you choose to eat.

Choosing between the junk and the genius is called your "taste" or your "gut." It's that still-small voice inside you that whispers in your ear: "This really stinks" or "This ain't bad." You may not be able to completely articulate why an idea is gold or lead, but most likely you will just feel the distinction. You can exercise great control over your information base and even the number of ideas you create, but the tricky thing is to decide which ones are worth pursuing.

Creativity beckons us to jump into the void—to shine a light into the darkness and risk following a new idea. You may find a good idea today that will seem half-baked tomorrow. You may discard an idea that comes back years later to haunt you. You may even create something that society tells you is total folly and then be discovered by generations to come as genius.

Pass the Genes, Please

Let's take a ridiculously broad sweeping perspective and consider for a moment where exactly we fit in the universe. The universe is basically a bunch of stars and planets floating around in a big black void as previously illustrated on my bedroom ceiling. In that universe there is a galaxy, and in that galaxy a star, and orbiting that star is earth and resting on earth is a highly sensitive, intuitive being prone to horrific acts of violence and unbelievable acts of kindness: Homo erectus—a term that was coined both to describe an advanced form of human life and to elicit chuckles in junior high school science classes throughout the world.

If viewed from outer space, this colony of about six billion humans may seem almost like a single cohesive organism. This organism of humanity is obsessed with building, crafting, and organizing the planet. Shaping, forming, interpreting, and studying the mysteries of life. Somewhere in this vast universe on this tiny planet is you. Feel pretty insignificant now, don't you?

What are we doing here? Why are we worried about Jerry Springer, global warming, and if our Olestra potato chips will give us gas? Why are we rushing around so much, trying to get ahead when such galactic forces are at work in the universe? We feel so tiny, almost like we are one small cell in the body of humanity, doing our job to service the body in our own small way for the betterment of the whole.

Our ancestors didn't seem to care much about the meaning of life when they grunted their way out of the primordial ooze. Their only concern seemed to deal with basic survival. But as their brains grew and their knuckles stopped dragging on the ground, the fundamentals of survival became second nature, and they longed for a sense of meaning and belonging in life. It wasn't enough just to build a fire and plow a field, they wanted to know where fire came from and why plants grow. Why were we put here in the first place and how can our voices be heard over the vast thunder of the cosmos?

We come from not only cosmic roots, but from a long human line of ancestors that ate, slept, laughed, cried, worked, and played their way through life just for a chance to pass their genes on to us. It seems funny in a way, because we are so much like our ancestors and we possess so many of their genetic gifts, and yet most of us can't say that we know a whole lot about them.

I know my grandpa was a mail carrier and my

grandma worked for the Burpee seed company. My grandpa liked to play cribbage and eat scallions with salt and my grandma made world-class rhubarb pie. My dad's mother was an interpreter during the Great War. She spoke four languages and would travel from her village in Poland to Krakow or Warsaw to interpret for the politicians and businessmen. She came to America with my dad and his cousins through Ellis Island in October 1921 and they all settled in Cleveland and later upstate New York.

I have some old photos of relatives from the nineteenth century. They seem nice enough even though I don't know much about them. I remember hearing talk about my great-great-grandmother who lived in Quincy, Illinois, and once served mashed potatoes to Abraham Lincoln. My great-grandfather published the German-speaking newspaper in Clinton, Iowa. I even remember meeting him when I was a little kid. He lived in a dark upstairs room in a big wooden house on Third Street in Clinton. There he would sit for hours on end doing what most men of his generation did—he smoked cigars and talked about politics. He looked like he was about five feet tall and he always wore a suit and tie—the same suit and tie that he wore in the picture I have.

I think about how we compare to his generation. We're taller and healthier now and I don't wear a tie as often. We probably smoke as many cigars but I really can't remember when I had a good long talk about politics. I think back about all of these strangers that are part of my family—that genetically live on in me—and I feel humbled.

We are alive in the most complex times. We're pretty lucky to be here at all. The fact that we were born was a million-to-one chance meeting between an egg and a sperm. The fact that we have survived infant disease, the cold war, junior high school dances, and disco is in and of itself reason to celebrate.

The truth is that you probably don't know very much about your own mom and dad much less the hundreds of ancestors who have lived their lives so that you could be here reading this book today. Their genetic inheritance is sitting inside you now. If you look closely you can see bits of Herman the miner and Aunt Rose the trollop. Grandpa Rudolph the tobacco farmer and Great-Great-Grandma Elsie the painter. Farther back there is Chester the horse thief and your medieval Uncle Heinz who supposedly went on the crusades and practiced witchcraft. These people all lived and loved and laughed and cried, and then they died. But they never died completely. They all passed a tiny portion of themselves on to you. They're all sitting right there in your lap in the form of genetic material—a vast storehouse of human potential sitting inside of us ready to be uncovered.

The same stunning system that has bred human beings into a billion different variations—from Stephen Hawking to Michael Jordan, from Einstein to Elvis—has bred you. Each relative, no matter how distant, threw something into the bag o' life that contributed to who you have become. Your oldest relatives were probably a pretty feeble bunch that spent most of their time dealing with life's basic problems, such as "maybe we can wear this" or "who wants to be the first to try eating that?" Our relatives of the Homo erectus persuasion may not have given us a specific genetic desire to wear animal skins, live in mud huts, and eat nuts, berries and the occasional woodpecker, but they did give us the gift of the survival instinct—the basic primal skill of knowing whether to fight or run and knowing that light usually means warmth and survival, and darkness means risk and possible demise.

Cave dwellers needed to exercise a certain amount of creative muscle just to survive. They fought to keep their fires burning in the dark, and to stay warm until the sunrise illuminated their life again. They knew the value of light. When you think about it, we really haven't changed much. We've merely exchanged the berries, loincloths, and mud huts of the past for Big Macs, Levi's, and a thirty-year mortgage. But even in our modern lives, we carry with us ancestral gifts, like our love of light and our desire to survive.

Dreamer, Doer

Our earliest predecessors were born with two sets of instructions in their brain. One set said: "Be conservative, save your energy, drink eight glasses of water, and wear a jacket before you go out." The other set of instructions said: "Go crazy, hurl yourself into life, drink eight glasses of beer, and wear a silly hat before you go out." Believe it or not, we need both of these instructions to live well, and while we all seem to get the first set of instructions loud and clear, we often deny the second set.

Yes, it seems like our craniums are occupied by a bickering odd couple who can't quite live with each other but can't live alone, either. Call them the dreamer and the doer. Our dreamer brain is visual, spatial, relational, nonverbal, and intuitive and loves to run, play, and watch reruns of *Green Acres*. It thinks in wild fantasies without reference to time, space, or the impending crisis in technology securities precipitated by the lower-than-forecasted third-quarter economic indicators. Our doer brain on the other hand *is* interested in third-quarter economic indicators and thrives on the structured, linear, logical, verbal, and analytic side of life. It is that pragmatic worker bee in all of us who busily goes about making lists, balancing checkbooks, sorting socks.

It's very hard to get the dreamer and doer to work in sync with each other. All too often we spend most of our day do, do, doing and a very small portion of the day dreaming. At other times we get lost in our thoughts and dream one set of dreams only to spend our waking hours doing something entirely different. Getting the dreamer and the doer to work together is one of the first baby steps toward reawakening the creative spirit.

It's no surprise that the doer in us often takes center stage. First consider the fact that in everyday life, a great portion of our waking hours are devoted to just keeping ourselves alive and well. Take a typical day and subtract the hours devoted to cooking, eating, cleaning, sleeping, shaving, shining, showering, plucking, waxing, and other unspeakable bodily functions. Then subtract occupational functions like commuting, meeting, memoing, calendar making, lunching, plucking, and waxing. Then finally subtract time spent shopping, taking the kids to school, picking up the dry cleaning, dropping the kids off at soccer, ballet, and the doctor. We're left with about thirty-nine seconds each day to be completely swept away in rapturous fantasy. You can begin to see that there is not a lot of leisure time left to even think about adding some creative balance to your life.

We lead lives of response. Response to emergencies, deadlines, doorbells, and telephones. As a result this deadening drone of life leaves us with little or no time for the dreamer. Creativity demands big protected chunks of time set aside just to dream, and big protected places like studios, labs, and libraries set aside just to dream in. Cultivating the dreamer is not just a once-in-a-while thing, but a constant, regular, habitual pattern of dreaming for the rest of our lives.

Toad's Brain

If you're like me, you are probably spending several hours a day wondering about the size of your brain. You're probably asking yourself right now, as people frequently do: Is my brain normal? Well, here's an interesting thought: The most accomplished neurosurgeon could open your skull right now and look at your brain and not really be able to distinguish it from the brain of Mozart, Einstein, or Crazy Guggenham. Brains are so similar in the amount of information they can process and the speed with which they can process it that one might hypothesize that we could all perform similar mental acrobatics at the level of the most accomplished scholars and artists.

Why then are there so many variations on human thought and accomplishment? Part of the answer comes down to a tally of how much time can truly be spent dealing with new thought and ideas. So much of our attention is consumed by survival activities, like eating and sleeping and working, that we're left with very little time for focused learning. There are moments in history when certain cultures were great breeding grounds of creative thought and action. Just think what it must have been like to be living in the highly creative cultures of ancient Greece, Florence in the Renaissance, or Paris during the nineteenth century.

These great epochs of creativity grew from times of relative prosperity when people had ample leisure time to devote to reading, painting, and debate. The personal challenge then is to carve out time for your own creative renaissance to take place. Time for your dreamer to dream deep, long, satisfying dreams.

My high school friend was named Toad (we never knew his real name or how he got the name Toad, but there are certain things in life that shouldn't be questioned). Toad was a fireplug of a boy. He was about five feet tall and spent the greater part of his high school years emitting vapors and making funny sounds with his hands. Other students had jammed their schedules with chess club, radio club, pep club, Latin club, and drill team and had very little time to devote to dreaming. Toad on the other hand had participated in none of these extracurricular activities and could devote large chunks of time thinking about:

- The mysteries of inner space.
- The vastness of the cosmos.
- How to line a locker with
  Vaseline and grass clippings.

The point is that we all have very real limitations to our time, and as such, limits on the number of things that we can attend to. But like Toad, we need to find a way to carve out time to follow our dreams.

Muskegon Conquered

It's only natural to want to emulate some of the great minds of the ages. In one way it's encouraging to think that human beings can rise to the heights of a Bach or a Baryshnikov; on the other hand it's intimidating to think of the accomplishments of highly creative people.

I hold up certain historical figures as my creative idols: Mozart, Beethoven, Ben Franklin, Chuck Dickens, Picasso, Groucho Marx, Frank Capra, Dorothy Kilgallen, Bennett Cerf, Kitty Carlisle Hart, Orson Bean. To tell the truth, I'm intimidated by their talent and accomplishment. How could anyone ever attain what these giants have attained? Why even try? But then I started to realize that many of these greats of history lived in a much smaller simpler world.

The Greeks didn't have much to work with but they did a lot for creativity in their era. In about 400 B.C., they began construction on the Parthenon, and the Greek mathematician Archytas invented the pulley and was credited with building the first heavier-than-air flying machine which, it was said, actually flew. Sophocles died around that time. He was a prize-winning wrestler and musician and was even a general in the Athenian army and he still had time left over to write one hundred twenty-three plays. The population of ancient Greece at that time was around three million people or roughly the size of greater Cleveland, Ohio. I'm in awe of this small culture that shaped the world and I expect a lot more from the citizens of Cleveland in the future.

In 43 A.D., the Romans, under direction of their emperor Claudius, occupied Britain and founded Londinium (London). The population of the British Isles was an estimated 800,000 people or about the combined size of modern-day Grand Rapids, Muskegon, and Holland, Michigan. Claudius was a fifty-three-year-old, short, balding Italian man not unlike Danny DeVito. Now I'm not saying that it

wouldn't be a newsworthy day if Danny DeVito invaded
Muskegon, or that Danny DeVito wouldn't make a heck
of an emperor, but the comparison does help us give human scale to the sometimes mythic events of history.

George Washington, Thomas Jefferson, John Adams,
and a group of upstart colonial businessmen played midwife to America in 1776. The population of the colonies
was 2,418,000, or about half the population of modern-day
Hong Kong. George was forty-four, John forty, and Tom
was a young thirty-three years old.

I don't mean to trivialize the accomplishments of these
giants of history, but this perspective helps me realize that
these historical figures lived in a very different world and
that they may have even put their pants on one leg at a
time.

We have such a leg up on our predecessors. We live in
an era of relative prosperity. One can not only dream of
affecting the entire world, but through the advance of the
information age, it's possible for an individual voice to be
heard around the world. We have incredible technology.
Dickens had no word processor, Mozart didn't have a syn-
thesizer or a sixty-four-track recording studio, the Roman
army didn't even own a Hummer.

Even though they lived in another world and their
technology was crude by today's standard, these historical
figures understood two timeless qualities that great innovators always seem to possess: a passion for ideas, and a
work ethic to carry them out. These are uniquely human
qualities. Our modern technology gives us neither. A generation ago, our parents had only a small black-and-white
television, no credit cards, and no Howard Stern, but they
put men on the moon with passion and work. At the end
of the nineteenth century, our parents' grandparents had

no airplanes, phones, lights, cars, or major-league baseball and yet in a span of forty years, all those things became reality with passion and work. History needs a human perspective. Don't be intimidated by it.

Nobody's Perfect

I was having a donut one day at a place called Fast Donut. I patronize Fast Donut because I believe it stands for the best that America has to offer. In Europe, you'd never see places like Fast Croissant or Fast Biscotti. Not only have we invented the donut, but we're happy to serve it to you fast. I like that.

Anyway, while I was waiting for my donut, I couldn't help overhearing the coffee-machine guy talking about the screenplay he was working on. Just the day before, I was having breakfast with a friend in a coffee shop and all the waiters and waitresses were talking about *their* screenplays—everyone in Los Angeles works on screenplays at night with the dream of making it big. There seems to be some link between screenwriting and places that serve breakfast food. I think they should just combine screenwriting and breakfast so that people like me could come in and hear waiters pitch you stories for new movies while you eat.

WAITER: Hi, my name's Eric and I'll be your server this morning. Today's special is the seafood omelet, and you'll be hearing a pitch for a premise starring Kevin Bacon.
PRODUCER: What's in it?
WAITER: Action, romance, pathos—

PRODUCER: No, what's in the omelet?

WAITER: Scallops, oysters, calamari . . .

PRODUCER: And what's today's pitch again?

WAITER: It's called *Briefcase* . . . it's a love story but from a completely different perspective. The film opens with a shot of a young lawyer named Brian Samson, played by . . .

PRODUCER: Kevin Bacon?

WAITER: Bingo.

PRODUCER: Could I order?

WAITER: Sure.

PRODUCER: Pancake sandwich with poached eggs and bacon.

WAITER: Coffee? (*Producer nods*) I'll be right back.

The waiter dashes over to another table to fill up their coffee cups and pitch Meryl Streep as the tortured wife of an NFL player in Personal Foul. *He returns.*

WAITER: Anyway, we think he'd be great.

PRODUCER: Who?

A busboy rifles past, plops down a tray of dishes, and whispers.

BUSBOY: Kevin Bacon.

PRODUCER: Oh.

WAITER: So . . . it's a story about this young lawyer who gets this job representing this transvestite guy who's accused of murder, and the media tries to make a mockery of the whole thing.

BUSBOY: Those bastards.

It is becoming increasingly apparent that the busboy is co-writing this screenplay.

PRODUCER: Really.

WAITER: The main character is this girl, only she's really a guy, and he's in a jail cell with Kevin Bacon and he's crying.

PRODUCER: Kevin Bacon?

BUSBOY: No, the guy . . . who's dressed like a girl.

PRODUCER: Really.

WAITER: Anyway, this transvestite admits to

murdering this other transvestite but he starts crying because, get this, because he was in love with the girl he murdered!

BUSBOY: Don't you get it?

PRODUCER: Get what?

WAITER: Two girls in love only they're guys!

PRODUCER: Well, how does Kevin Bacon feel?

WAITER: About what?

PRODUCER: About what! He's in a jail cell with a girl who's really a guy that killed a guy who's dressed like a girl! Don't you think he'd have an opinion about all this?!!?

WAITER: Well . . . he's confused.

PRODUCER: No foolin'.

The waiter exits over to the counter where he chats hurriedly with a young girl, who has been hearing his pitch for King Lear in Space. *He shoots the producer an "I'll-be-right-with-you" glance and returns with his coffee.*

WAITER: So now Kevin Bacon knows she's guilty but he still has to defend her, and his dilemma is he's falling in love with her.

PRODUCER: But she's a guy.

BUSBOY: (*yelling from across the restaurant*) He doesn't know that!!

PRODUCER: He doesn't know that!?!

WAITER: He thinks the guy is the most beautiful and vulnerable girl he's ever met. *He* thinks she's a girl, but *we* know she's a guy. So, here's the topper: he goes to court the next day after a long night of preparation and he's really struggling with his feelings for her and now it's the first day of the trial, she's ushered into the courtroom, only—get this—now she's dressed like a guy!

The busboy has joined the waiter and producer now along with a waitress and one of the owners, all gathered around with a yer-gonna-love-this-part grin.

BUSBOY: Now Kevin Bacon thinks, Holy shit, she's a guy.

WAITER: He'll cough up a lung!

WAITRESS: Who wouldn't.

WAITER: So, the guy comes in and sits next to Kevin Bacon, who has had the shock of his life and can't say anything about it 'cause the trial is about to begin. All the guy does is lean over, like that guy at the end of *Some Like It Hot,* and says, "Nobody's perfect!"

The gathering breaks into uncontrollable laughter.

BUSBOY: Get it! It's an homage!

PRODUCER: Wow.

WAITER: Well, there it is . . . what do you think?

(Producer exudes half-compliments.)

PRODUCER: I've never heard anything quite like it . . . leave it to you to come up with something like this . . . unbelievable . . . it's gonna be huge.

I like waiters who write screenplays. I like people who spend their off-hours writing late into the night on the one chance that their story will make it to the screen. It's hard to be dismissive of the passion and work ethic that these midnight warriors possess.

And who's to say that someday their work won't make one heck of a movie. *E.T., Forrest Gump,* and *Beauty and the Beast* were all bypassed or shelved at different studios. They were all dismissed at one time or another and only got made through the passion and hard work of the film-makers. I'm sure by now that the coffee guy at Fast Donut has a development deal at a major studio. Why not, and Kevin Bacon if you're reading this, please stay by your phone.

Artifacts

As hard as you may try, you can't guarantee a positive reaction to your personal brand of creativity. For every successfully produced screenplay, there are thousands of scripts that languish in the bottoms of drawers and on dusty shelves, never to see the light of day again. We live in a society that values and rewards success. This can lead you to be a very success-driven artist, which in turn can lead you to be constantly disappointed. Creative expressions rarely succeed financially and you can't always measure the value of a creation by the yardstick of success.

Van Gogh painted an undistinguished and anonymous lifetime before he died in obscurity. His work went on to be the most celebrated among the impressionists. Mozart was a musical genius and was buried in a pauper's common grave. People hated *Moby Dick* when it was published and the early episodes of *Seinfeld* garnered some of the most dismal ratings in television history in a year that was dominated by the number-one show *Jake and the Fatman*.

What then do Vincent, Wolfgang, Herman, and Jerry have in common? The drive to create regardless of the outcome. They were driven to paint, compose, write, and tell jokes at any cost. To live a life that was committed to their craft day in and day out, regardless of the perceived success or failure of their work.

Our capitalist system loves and rewards tangible success. We attain that success by a system based on ideas, products, deadlines, and money. We judge our success or failures by how we meet deadlines, how good the product is, and how big the financial rewards are.

We are completion oriented. We learn to celebrate the

arrival of a deadline with pomp and circumstance. The arrival of a product with headlines and hyperbole. There's even a trend in some businesses to celebrate the beginning of an undertaking. But nobody wants to celebrate the process.

This obsession with the end product sets us up for a nasty lifelong pattern of long periods of boredom, stress, and tension while waiting to celebrate, followed by a short celebration, followed by long periods of boredom, stress, and tension, and so on. Not a fun way to spend life.

The process is where the treasure of creativity is buried. It's the feeling you get when you are immersed in a project with your head down and all one billion brain cells are immersed in trying to forge idea, craft, and medium into a new creation on a canvas, or in a laboratory, or in a saucepan.

Think of any creative production as you would a big vacation. When we take a long trip to London, for example, our journey will take us to charming shops, pubs, quaint hotels, pubs, restaurants, pubs, landmarks, and pubs, and we'll be totally immersed in all order of interesting and memorable things along the way. In fact, we form memories that last a lifetime on trips like this. The literal goal of your trip was to travel to London and return home in two weeks. When we arrive home we would never say, "Thank God I met my deadline of returning home in two weeks."

When we return, we find how completely absorbed we were by our journey. We love to recount the joy, pain, elation, and disappointment along the way. At the end of our trip, we revel in the journey—not the deadline of arriving home.

We show the stupid pictures of us in front of everything. We wax sentimental about the charming bobby who clamped our rental car when we parked illegally in front of Harrods. We shake our heads as we recount the time we locked ourselves in our hotel room with a bottle of Old Bushmills and some Slim Jims and watched *Fawlty Towers* reruns. We toss our heads back and laugh like Errol Flynn when we tell the story about the time we had too many beers and did the full monty in the taxi queue in front of the House of Commons. The arrival home means very little, the journey means everything. A creative journey is the same.

There is no assurance of success, acknowledgment, fame, fortune, respect, or cash prizes at the end of our creative process. There is nothing in life that guarantees us a place in immortality. Even fame in our own time doesn't guarantee us that. The famous people of a century ago are all but forgotten. The only thing we have is our present moment, and the incredibly joyful feeling we experience when we are working in our favorite craft and solving the problems that our project presents to us. Enjoy the journey along your creative highway like a dog with his head out the window of a car—eyes wide open, ears back, nose wet, completely absorbed.

When you focus on the journey and not the arrival, then your art becomes more like a treasured artifact of the creative process. A painting, a poem, a sketch, or a piece of music that you've written becomes a record of your life—a souvenir of the creative process, just as much as the photos are an artifact of your unforgettable travels abroad.

The Truth and Some Lies

Attribution means a lot in the art world. Imagine two equally beautiful paintings hung side by side in a gallery. One has a plaque that says Rembrandt and the other says Buddy Flubson. Even if they were both masterful paintings, I'm sure I'd like the Rembrandt more than the Buddy Flubson. I'd feel drawn to it because of the attribution to a well-known artist.

There are dozens of self-help books in the world of business where you can find pithy quotes attributed to great men and women. There are quite a few quotes in this book. These are quotes from smart people, quotes from people who have "done it" before, quotes from people who think they know what they are doing, and quotes of great inspiration and valor.

Some people are quoted more than others. Einstein and Picasso fall into this category. Picasso, by the way, hated to be quoted so you'll notice that I've quoted him about nine hundred times in this book. If you disregard the fact that his behavior was, by all accounts, appalling and his personal life was a disaster, he actually had some interesting things to say about art and creativity.

People love to hear what big, influential, successful artists have to say. Here's another quote from a very famous person:

> There will be those who say that it can't be done. Those who would try and stop us, but we must persevere knowing that God is with us.
>
> —Franklin Delano Roosevelt

These are inspirational words indeed. So inspirational in fact that they would be equally as good coming from a football coach:

> There will be those who say it can't be done. Those who would try and stop us, but we must persevere knowing that God is with us.
>
> —NOTRE DAME FOOTBALL COACH KNUTE ROCKNE

Or a religious leader:

> There will be those who say it can't be done. Those who would try and stop us, but we must persevere knowing that God is with us.
>
> —BILLY GRAHAM

But the same words can be chilling if ascribed to a despot:

> There will be those who say it can't be done. Those who would try and stop us, but we must persevere knowing that God is with us.
>
> —ADOLF HITLER

The words themselves are identical but your impression of the words are completely changed by the attribution. Roosevelt's quote seems like it must refer to the war effort. Coach Rockne's is obviously a halftime pep talk to his fighting Irish. Billy Graham offers a spiritual hope for all of us, and Hitler's quote seems like the obvious ravings of a misguided madman. Attribution sways our point of view.

It's like those stories you hear from time to time about a person finding a Rembrandt etching at a garage sale. One day the sketch was a worthless piece of paper up for sale for fifty cents along with the old skis and the blacklight Jimi Hendrix poster. The next day it was a new-found treasure of the art world worth hundreds of thousands of dollars. Same piece of art, different attribution.

All of this rush to associate a painting with a great artist or a quote with an exceptional person is fine, but try once to take a step away from the fame or attribution of a piece of art and instead form your own opinion regarding that art. Be critical. Be introspective. Be honest. Just because a painting hangs in a museum, doesn't mean you have to like it. Just because a famous person is quoted, doesn't mean it has relevance to your life. Not all novels by Steinbeck, plays by Tennessee Williams, or films by Hitchcock are uniformly brilliant. You may adore some and feel ambivalent toward others. Be critical about what you observe. Disregard pedigree and form an opinion based on how you feel about something and not on the attribution of a piece of art or music to a certain expert or master. Celebrate Buddy Flubson. Find a Picasso that you hate, some Mozart that doesn't work for you, a classic movie that everyone else loves, but that you find flawed. Find an obscure artist to embrace, an unknown band whose music you love, and a little-known film that moves you deeply.

The truth and beauty of art is in the eyes of the beholder. What you see as truth may be a lie to me. You may see a hero and I see a goat. You may see artistic brilliance and I see nothing.

The attribution of a quote, a painting, a poem is indeed important. Knowing that a painting was by Jackson Pollock helps us understand him and his place in our culture and makes it more than just some accidental splats of paint. But the real truth is how a quote, a painting, or a poem speaks to you personally. Does it move you deeply? Does it engage your imagination? Does it challenge your beliefs?

Here's a list of age-old quotes that have no attribution. These pithy little sayings are powerful on their own without knowing who said them because they each represent a little capsule of human wisdom. These couplets do, however, contradict one another, and so just when you find a quote to support your point of view, alongside is a quote of equal weight that will undercut your point of view entirely.

Look before you leap.
He who hesitates is lost.
If at first you don't succeed, try, try again.
Don't beat your head against a stone wall.
Absence makes the heart grow fonder.
Out of sight, out of mind.
Two hands are better than one.
Paddle your own canoe.
Haste makes waste.
Time waits for no man.
You're never too old to learn.
You can't teach an old dog new tricks.
It's better to be safe than sorry.
Nothing ventured, nothing gained.
Hitch your wagon to a star.
Don't bite off more than you can chew.
Many hands make light work.
Too many cooks spoil the broth.
Don't judge a book by its cover.
Clothes make the man.
The squeaking wheel gets the grease.
Silence is golden.

Never put off till tomorrow what you can do today.
Don't cross the bridge till you come to it.

The Pursuit of Happiness

Thomas Jefferson rented a room once in Philadelphia and locked himself in with a pot of tea, his violin, some pens, some paper, a bottle of Old Bushmills, and some Slim Jims . . . oh sorry, I got confused there for a minute. In any case, two days later he emerged with a document declaring the colonies' independence from George III. Like most Americans, I had read the Declaration of Independence in school or heard bits of it quoted during patriotic demonstrations, but I had never really appreciated Jefferson's definition of freedom until recently. He says:

> We hold these truths to be self-evident, that all men are created equal, that they are endowed by their creator with certain unalienable rights, that among these are life, liberty, and the pursuit of happiness.

To the colonials this was pretty great stuff (especially if you were a white man, since women and people of color didn't enjoy the same benefits until much much later). What Jefferson was able to do was to define freedom in a very abstract, rhapsodic way that we could all agree on. The truth probably is that freedom doesn't always mean equality and equality doesn't always foster the spirit of happiness. What I like about this sentence is the simplicity of its truth: We are all created equal to pursue our own lives, freedom, and happiness.

The pursuit of happiness is an idea that comes from Aristotle. He thought that all human strivings and yearnings could be distilled down to one thought: All we want is dark chocolate. Well, actually he said that all we want is to achieve happiness, but I frequently confuse the two. There are a million ways to be happy; the pursuit of a creative dream is one of them.

Once, at the end of a long work day, my phone rang and it was one of the assistant production managers asking if he could come up and talk. Let's call him Sven Bjornson since I don't want to reveal his true identity and I adore the sound of Scandinavian names. "Sure," I said, and in a few minutes Sven walked into my office, closed the door, and sat down.

"I need some advice." He had been doing his job in junior management for a long time and you could tell that something was starting to nag at him. Sven wanted to do what everyone else in Hollywood wants to do, he wanted to write screenplays. He was taking a class in screenwriting and had begun writing a screenplay but he felt stuck and wanted a push in the right direction.

"Sven," I said in a paternal tone, "you can either tiptoe into the shallow end or jump naked into the deep end. It all depends how much you want to swim."

If you are going to pursue your happiness, you must start by deciding what your happiness is. What's inside of you? What story do you have to tell? What truth do you have to share? The most successful writers write because they have to. They have an unquenchable burning desire to write about the world through their eyes. Picasso said that a painter doesn't paint because he or she wants to, but rather because they have to to unload themselves of life's impressions. This whole conversation with Sven really came down to how much Sven really *had* to write.

If Sven was willing to go home at night and say to

himself, I'm going to work harder than anyone else, I'm
going to carve out big chunks of time to write and study
films and scripts and commit myself to my passion, then
maybe he would get a break and be able to write a magazine article that would lead to a television movie and then
a feature. Otherwise, he'd be a hobbyist for life. Not a bad
thing, but an amateur thing. It's the difference between the
weekend golfer and Tiger Woods.

Then Sven said something that stopped me. He was
talking about his high school and that every day he was
doing something different in drama or art or music and
that when he came to work in management he left all that
behind him. He decided years ago to put his dream on a
shelf for a while, but he never went back to it. In essence
he was living a lie by denying himself the parts of his life
that gave him joy. Whole areas that he once loved in his
high school life now lie dormant and undeveloped.

Sven was at a crossroads. Most people who come to
this intersection won't make a dramatic change. They may
take a class, practice a bit, and then see the writing on the
wall and pull the plug on their dreams once again. One
percent will latch onto the dream like a bear trap and not
let go. They will work and seek out experts and study and
marry their dream for better or worse, richer or poorer, in
sickness and in health, till death do us part. They will work
to dig deeply for the truth about their lives. To explore
their desire to create without guilt and for no other reason
than this: because they have to.

If you love your dream, why not marry it? Feel the fire
in your gut. Grit your teeth, put your ears back, and
scream a primal scream. There is strength in boldness and
let's face it, the alternative doesn't sound very satisfying.

Pursue happiness. Strip down and dive into the deep

end with Sven. The water is deep, cool, and endlessly refreshing and you've got plenty of strength to swim to
shore.

Thinking Outside the Box

I loved being a Cub Scout. I loved the snappy blue uniforms, the sharp blue caps, and the crisp yellow neckerchief. I loved the word *neckerchief*. Life in Cub Scouts meant
weekly pack meetings at Mr. and Mrs. Gillan's house. We
never went inside the house, but always had our meetings
at a picnic table in the garage alongside the power mower,
bikes, and bags of manure. A typical meeting would start
with the pledge of allegiance and the Cub Scout oath and
then proceed into any number of boy-pleasing crafts.

Once we made Christmas trees out of an old *Reader's
Digest* magazine by folding the corners of all the pages into
the center spine. Another time we made pinewood derby
racers. All pinewood derby racers start with identical
boxed kits that include a ten-inch chunk of wood, a set of
plastic wheels, and some rudimentary hardware. Each cub
then went home and started whittling away, with Mom
and Dad's help, to build their own personalized custom
racer.

On race day, everyone showed up with their completed car. Some had beautiful paint jobs, and others had
flames and that stupid woodpecker-smoking-a-cigar decal.
The scouts would line up their racers on a track made of
parallel lanes of plywood and they'd race in heats. The
fastest cars were the ones that took advantage of gravity
by putting weights in front of their cars, but whatever the
modifications, the cars had to be built with only the con-

tents supplied in the box and in strict compliance with long-standing rules set by the Boy Scouts of America.

Toad walked in the door with a big grin on his face, cradling his pinewood derby racer in both hands. He had completely hollowed out his race car body to look like a scud missile launcher and then strapped his brother's eighteen-inch solid-fuel model rocket to the chassis. Then he painted a big U.S. flag and the words TO HONOR AMERICA on the side of the fuselage. I was pretty sure Toad hadn't looked at the rules.

His car was the hands-down sentimental favorite with the entire troop, but was disqualified on the grounds that it was a dangerous nuisance. Days later, we gave it a test run by lighting it up on the school playground. It took off with unimaginable speed, ricocheted off the bicycle racks, shot across the softball field, and blew up in a huge ball of flames inside the third-base dugout. The whole trip took about two seconds. The wheels never really touched the ground. Toad was beside himself with joy and I had just had my first real experience with someone who thought outside the box.

Not long after that, I graduated to Boy Scouts where I noticed a change. The uniforms were now green with a red neckerchief and the older boys looked much older indeed. One of the older scouts, named Mitch, even shaved and talked about girls. Cub Scouts was easy because we all did the same crafts and read the same stories. In Boy Scouts, we were free to explore who we were and what we liked. Boy Scouts even offered a variety of merit badges representing lots of ways a young lad like me could express himself in all his glorious pubescence.

There were the standard sort of badges for hiking and camping, canoeing and fishing. There were merit badges for personal fitness, personal finance, and salesmanship. They had badges for rural things like forestry, soil conservation, hog production, and sheep farming. There were police-prep badges like marksmanship and fingerprinting. Badges for those with artistic aspirations like painting, sculpting, and basket weaving. Badges with lofty and altruistic sounding names like "citizenship in the home" and "world brotherhood." Everyone could express his strength and get a badge as recognition (with the exception of Toad, who desperately wanted a merit badge for sleeping bag flatulence, which we eventually gave him).

Merit badges were a good idea. I wish they still handed them out to adults. It'd be a real ice-breaker at parties. When you met someone, you could just look down at their green sash and say, "I can't help but notice that you're into hog production."

I wonder what our adult merit badges would look like? Net surfing, freeway commuting, beer swilling? Garage hoarding, procrastination, highest calorie consumption in one sitting?

In scouting, even as young men, we wore these badges as a sign of who we were. The number of badges you wore showed diversity of interest and commitment to learning. I sometimes stop and think about the merit badges I earned so many years ago. What others have I earned . . . really earned . . . since then? What merit badges would you give yourself, or do you need to start earning some?

Labels

A few years back after watching Kevin Costner in *Dances with Wolves*, I became fascinated with the Native American way of selecting names. It seemed so honest and forthright to have a name like Runs with the Wind or Dancing Bear. It was much more poetic than the names that the people in my neighborhood had: Our insurance man was simply called Fred Field, and our family stockbroker had the utilitarian name Steve Johnson. Why couldn't they be like the Indians and have a little poetry in their names: Fred Fiddles with Actuaries or Steve Runs with Bull Markets.

I started to take stock of the people around me as if they were Native Americans, wondering what their names would be.

At work I encountered my colleague, a famous animator whom I now call Walks with Donut and his assistant who commuted to work I would dub Drives with Travel Mug. The staff secretary Whopping Big Hair says hello to me on her way to set up a meeting with her boss, Runs with Giants and an executive from a well-known Hollywood studio Yells on Cell Phone.

I surveyed people away from the workplace and found Flirts with Firemen, and Skirt Chaser. At the supermarket I saw Waits for Parking Space.

I apply my same native American yardstick to my dad, who is now Drives with Turn Signal On and my neighbor who would be Peers Through Windows and her husband, Laughs No More. I wave hello to my good friend down the street who takes his poodle for a run each morning. His name is Jogs with Crapping Dog.

It was hard coming up with a name for myself but after much soul searching, I settled upon Awakes with Tongue on Floor.

We humans love labels. We label our clothes and our food and our freeways and our politicians. We put extra labels on hot dogs, cereal, and record albums: 97% Fat-Free, Toy Inside, 10% More.

We label movies with ratings: PG-13, parental guidance recommended. Television programs warn "not suitable for children with small families" (or is it the other way around?). I always find it odd that we'll rate a movie based solely on the amount of language, sex, and violence. Why stop there? It seems to me that we should rate everything about a movie. If I can pick up a can of Spam at the supermarket and read the entire contents, why shouldn't I be able to read the contents of a movie off the movie poster? Like food ingredients, you could list the good and the bad: "Contains: strong language, violence, stupid dialogue in the second act, a meaningless love story that seems pasted on, but there is a cool dinner scene where a girl eats a whole lobster with her bare hands."

We love to affix labels to everything, but most of all we love to label ourselves. We put ourselves into neat little boxes for classification, not unlike a butterfly collection. He's a teacher, she's an insurance saleswoman, he's a thespian, she's a lesbian, he's a liberal, she's a conservative. Teacher, salesman, liberal—all pretty generic labels for complex human beings. The labels deceive us because the saleswoman is also an actress, a writer, and a weekend gardener and the teacher is not just a teacher, but also an artist, a singer, and a weekend hockey goalie.

There seems to be a need for our tidy doer brain to categorize everything. Even random grasses and wildflowers can be neatly sorted into kingdom, phylum, class, order, family, genus, and species. But imagine for a moment what would happen if those labels didn't exist. What if words didn't define. Instead of the "anglo, middle-aged, Catholic, rock hound," you would just be : . . you, the individual. In truth you *are* an individual in every way. Nobody does it, sees it, wears it, eats it, learns it, and creates it the way you do.

What if the labels were off and it was just you the spirit. You the pumping heart, the breathing lungs, the aching back. Just you.

What Do You Live For?

Being on the tightrope is living; everything else is waiting.

—KARL WALLENDA

Now that the labels are off, who exactly are you? What are you good at? What do you love to do? What is your fatal flaw? What is your flame, your torch, your favorite condiment? What will be your creative gift to the world? Look carefully. The answer doesn't lie in what your dad or mom wanted you to do, or in what your partner wants you to do, but in what *you* want to do. And remember, we are not talking about your career or job, but your life. In searching for your own personal gift, don't feel like you are limited to an occupation.

Here's an example: Even though I hate to quantify creative achievement, every March I celebrate my hypocrisy, don my tuxedo, and go to the Academy Awards ceremony in Hollywood. There amid the limos, movie stars, shouting fans, and cleavage I see my old friend from college, Dave. Dave valet parks cars for a living. He works for the company that parks your car on Oscar night. Dave also happens to be a world-class organ player. Pipe organ.

Big wonderful pipes and pedals with stacks and stacks of keyboards. He is gifted and passionate about playing the organ and he knows it. Dave also runs a valet parking service. The point is, Dave *lives* to play the organ not to park your Cutlass. What do *you* live for? Only you can decide. Do you want to direct a movie? Do you want buns of steel? That small voice inside of you that helps you gravitate toward cooking or poetry, finance or beaver husbandry is the very thing that makes you unique. Take the limitations away, take the labels off, and pick your passion.

Sometimes it helps to imagine what your view will be like from the end of your life. What will it feel like looking back over the years? What will your proudest accomplishments be? Raising children, creating a business, writing poems. What will be your biggest regret? Never learning to play piano, not traveling to Rome, never learning to fly-fish, write, or cook a quiche. Now, back up from the end of your life to today. It doesn't matter if you are eighty-five or twenty-five, you have one thing on your side: You are alive. With the remainder of your life, you have the complete control to move some things from the regret column to the accomplishment column. Pursue your happiness.

When you finally choose your muse, you may struggle with the feeling that your chosen field is insignificant or has little value. We create in a world that tells us all things are not equal. It's a world that seems to reward success in a big way—a world that likes to keep score on achievement. Your house, your car, your education, your clothes, your job, all scream out loud about you and where you fit into the hierarchy of society.

We put creative achievements into the same type of

hierarchy where we rank some things to be of more importance than others. But what if creativity had no hierarchy? There is an impulsive desire in all of us to quantify creative achievement—to attach a value on a person's gift. For example, we generally feel like actors and film directors are more creative than salespeople or body-shop owners. We like to rank chefs, artists, athletes, and executives. Who is the best actor? What is the best picture of the year? Book of the year? Play of the year?

But on a fundamental level there is great value and nobility in all creative processes. The *Mona Lisa* has value and so does the painting of those dogs playing poker. An episode of *60 Minutes* and an episode of *South Park* both have value. You might prefer one or the other but you can't presuppose that one has value and one doesn't. Each grows from culture. Each contributes to culture. Each reflects and in a way defines culture.

Artists, musicians, chefs, and architects struggle constantly with thoughts that their work may or may not have value or social relevance. It can become an obstacle to feeling satisfied with your own work. As much as we may look to culture to validate us, no one can really tell you if your work has value or not. No one but you.

The Highly Creative Person

The desire to create is a uniquely human sport. Sure, the animals may build the occasional nest or dam up the occasional stream. But you never see a cow writing a script or a chimp acting (well, almost never). Humans create constantly, but some people excel. Some create with astounding brilliance. What is it that we can learn from highly creative people? What do they have in common? It's many things.

Some of the most brilliantly creative people on the planet live lives of paradox. At times they are physical and vigorous and at other times quiet and contemplative. At times they are expansive and playful and at other times surgically focused and disciplined. Highly creative people have the willingness to spend limitless time on an idea and come up blank. They have the audacity to throw themselves into unknown ventures and risk spectacular failure. They live in a world of boundless imagination and sobering reality.

Creative people are both extroverts and introverts. Social and solitary. Humble and proud. They are both student and teacher. Creative people even seem both male and female and are able to escape many gender-established cultural expectations. They tend toward a kind of psychological androgyny that allows them to feel emotions that might be considered solely male (aggression, rigidity) or female (passivity, sensitivity). This openness to the psychological arsenal of both sexes can allow the artist to interpret the world with a much larger emotional vocabulary.

Creative people are products of tradition. Some seem eccentric and full of rebellion. They may shout profanities, belch in public, and lick their guitar strings but even the most rebellious jerk is first and foremost rooted in an incredibly traditional world. The music of the Squirrel Nut Zippers—a kind of zydeco-swing-polka rock—is rooted not only in folk and rock music but also in the musical foundations laid by Bach and Buxtehude three centuries ago.

Creative people have an historical awareness. When Julie Taymor adapted *The Lion King* for the Broadway stage, her visionary approach to the material created a version of the story that is stunning and unforgettable, but the roots of the production lie in centuries-old traditions from countries around the world. It grows from the soil of animation, of Broadway theater, of Javanese shadow puppetry, of Japanese Bunraku puppetry, of modern dance, and of African tribal chant. Julie's genius is how she chose to bring all of these elements together to create a new visual tapestry that is like nothing you've ever seen before.

To be creative is to be totally and passionately committed to your work—to be in love with your work and yet be able to separate yourself from it enough to hate it. It means to be completely attached to what you are doing and then becoming completely detached so you can criticize yourself. It is a life of pain and vulnerability, of elation and ecstasy. To be creative is to live a life of contradiction. This story, however, has a trick ending.

Here's the twist: There is no reason why this "highly creative person" can't be you. Certainly your life is at times physical and vigorous and at other times quiet and contemplative. At times you may be expansive and playful and at other times surgically focused and disciplined. I'm sure you've spent limitless time on an idea and come up blank, and who doesn't live in a world of boundless imagination tempered with sobering reality.

My drawing teacher told me a story about a student of his who struggled and agonized over his drawings. They were stiff and unsure. The teacher talked to the student after class and said, "You know, your drawings are stiff and unsure because you are stiff and unsure. You have to start thinking like an artist—believing you're an artist. Engage your mind first and your drawings will follow."

When you read about the "highly creative person" it's easy to think of that person as someone else. We jump at the chance to celebrate the creativity of others, yet we stop short of celebrating the creative spirit that lies within ourselves. Every trait of a highly creative person is a trait that you possess. The challenge is to engage your mind and start thinking of that highly creative person as you.

Access

Our human condition is based on access. Our ancestors survived because they had access to food and shelter. They may have excelled because they had access to the best books and universities. We are restricted or set free by our ability to access things—knowledge, information, political power, dark chocolate. In our pursuit of Aristotle's happiness, one way or another what we all need is access.

Business is built on access to people, ideas, money, and the marketplace. If I can get access to some clever and interesting people, they will come up with an idea that will allow me access to some money from the bank, which will allow me to manufacture my idea and advertise it, to try to access the consumer in the marketplace. At any step along the way, if I am denied access either to the people, the idea, the money, or the market, I won't be doing so well. Access is everything.

If I want to make a movie, I need access to the best directors and the biggest stars. If I have access to Harrison Ford, then I will probably get access to the money and the distribution of the film. I probably won't have quite the same situation if I have access to, say, Frank Stallone, but then again, you never know.

Historically, people get and hold power by controlling access. This worked for Alexander the Great, Napoleon, Attila the Hun, and Bill Gates (not to imply that these four gentlemen have anything in common). The rich and powerful of history knew that to maintain their edge, they had to deprive both their competitors and the common man of any access to other ideas, information, or money lest the latter gain a foothold.

Taken to extreme, political revolution has resulted when the people have demanded access to information, power, or truth. The French, American, and Russian revolutions sprang from a desire for access.

For centuries, artists, writers, filmmakers, and even comedians have opened people's eyes to oppression and given the audience access to new ways of thought.

When Picasso painted his requiem for the bombed and burned Basque town of Guernica, he was opening our eyes to the horrors of war. When Dickens wrote *A Christmas Carol*, he educated the growing Victorian middle class in England on how to behave during the holidays. Upton Sinclair's *The Jungle*, Robert Altman's *M*A*S*H*, Steven Spielberg's *Schindler's List*, the comedy of Lenny Bruce or Mort Sahl all brought social issues to the public in sometimes shocking but always accessible ways. The creative community has always been at the forefront of the demand for access.

Access has another more personal effect on life. We are in the midst of an unusual time in history when information is more readily available than ever before. There was a time only recently when the type of books, media, and art that were available to you depended upon where you lived. If you lived in Bellflower, you had fewer opportunities to access information than if you lived in Paris or

New York. If you lived in a rural area, you had less access than in the city.

Access is still an issue, but things are beginning to change. People who live in the most remote sections of the planet can have access, with the aid of a computer and a phone line, to nearly every book, article, painting, and photograph known to mankind.

In the middle ages, there was virtually no access to information unless you worked for royalty or the church. Then the advent of the printing press and movable type spawned an information boom. Even one generation ago, if you were economically underprivileged, disabled, or a single parent raising a child at home, it would have taken a Herculean effort to access any meaningful quantity of information from beyond your local library. Now we have the promise of a world where nearly anyone, if they have the resources, can access information from anywhere.

The foundation of higher creativity is learning and learning comes from information. We have access to information and so we have access to the building blocks of creativity. The only remaining obstacle is a personal one. We need to find the time—make the time—to learn. If your field is painting, finance, cooking, dance, music, whatever, the barriers to access are being removed and the opportunity to learn, and hence to create, has never been better.

Words

The Internet represents a return to the printed word in the aftermath of the video-centric life of the television era. Although images will always provide a primary source of communication, words are also a common currency of creative communication and so we need to discuss them and their usage. Words are a very unusual commodity. They are pure symbolism. The word *liberty*, for example, symbolizes a grand and abstract concept of humanity in a fairly simple seven letters. Love is a highly symbolic word, too, as is the word *family*. They are words that are charged with meaning.

The names we give to people, places, and things are symbolic, too. We give some things, like foods, rather simple, serious-sounding names: potatoes, beef, ham, rice. There are other foods that we have given silly-sounding names: cauliflower, kiwi, monkfish, and kumquats. Sometimes two serious words combine to make one silly-sounding name like passion fruit, mistletoe, or beernuts.

Some activities can't be described with just one word and so we've invented countless alternatives. For example, one can be drunken, soused, blitzed, smashed, pickled, pissed (English), besotted, crapulent, crapulous, or inebriated. And one can vomit, barf, disgorge, heave, puke, retch, spew, throw up, call Ralph, call Rourke, call Buick, blow chunks, Technicolor yawn, and talk to God on the big white phone. Other human activities are so basic that they can only be described in one perfect and all-inclusive word. For example: polka.

Words fall easily into groups and we like that. Words on a similar subject create a feeling of topical familiarity when grouped together. For example, there are lists of:

- Words of rest: safe, home,
  friend, dad, beer, eat, bed, nap
- Words of unrest: crazy, lunatic,
  insane, nuts, wacko, mad, odd

- Words of undress: panties,
  PJs, undies, T-shirts, briefs,
  boxers
- Affectionate words: kiss, hug,
  squeeze, cuddle, embrace
- Big-concept words: life, light,
  love, devotion, loyalty
- Spiritual words: god, faith,
  spirit, angel, soul, hymn, holy
- Confrontation words: fight,
  yell, hit, slug, shout, push
- Words of trust: promise,
  guarantee, assure, insure, safe
- Words of mistrust: fraud,
  fake, phony, bogus, slimeball,
  sleazebag
- Shopping words: bargain,
  shop, sale, item, buy, tag, price
- Words of appeal: beg, plead,
  cajole, implore, pray

Like a painter composes a painting for visual effect, the way in which a writer groups words together into sentences will make us feel comfortable or uncomfortable depending on the assembly of words. A sentence, for example, with groups of words on the same topic is rarely shocking or insightful. Here's a sentence about shopping that contains no surprises:

> When I shop for a bargain, I always look for a sale item
> to buy or at least check the tag for the best price.

Well then, that certainly was a perfectly useful combination of words without much tension. You can make a sentence a little more interesting by using the words from opposing topics. Here's an example using words about rest and unrest together in the same sentence:

> It sounds crazy, but I always feel oddly safe at home drinking beer with my wacko dad.

It makes sense and communicates the idea completely with a little tension and poetry. In order to create unrest with words, let's combine some words, still from the lists above, but in a random and unexpected way that mixes words from many groups with an unsettling unexpected effect:

> I felt crazy sitting home in my undies yelling a hymn at God, begging him to guarantee me life.

Each word pulls us in a different direction. The combination of words is unexpected and so it makes you listen and try to understand. There is an uncomfortable tension about these words. Here are some more provocative thoughts using word couplets that contradict and inspire us to think:

> I yelled at the insane angel that was my dad. His life was a mad fraud, a holy home for beer and bogus devotion.

In this way, words are more than just a necessary conduit for communication. They become a medium to express complex emotions. Like oil paint and clay, they can be molded and manipulated so that they can express thoughts and tensions that supersede the literal meanings of the words. Jack Kerouac would be proud.

The symbolic quality of words extends into the names we have chosen for our world. A name is an incredibly powerful label that can conjure up deep feelings. We're not

so willing to give our children silly names. We prefer pop-
ular and noble names like Matthew, Jason, Caroline, and
Brittany, instead of names like Stumpy, Toad, and Moon
Unit.

And who wouldn't want to be friends with the Good-
man family, the Dearborns, or the Brainard family. Yet
we're not as sure about Steve and Cindy Houndsditch, Bob
and Sally Plotz, or the Judas family.

When developers name their housing tracts, they draw
on word-based images that evoke comfort and peace. It's
easy to name a housing development. First pick a word
from the left side of this list and then join it with any word
from the right side of the list to create a name for your
new hometown:

North	brook
South	hills
East	peak
West	ranch
Fox	tree
Saddleback	ridge
Oak	park
Sunset	pines

Wouldn't you be happy living in Northhills, Foxbrook,
or Saddleback Peak? I'd love to shop at the Oakpark Mall.
And for extra credit, just add the word *Estates* after your
new name. It makes anything sound more classy: Saddleback Peak Estates. These words conjure up home and
hearth much more than Monkeyditch, Devil's Crotch, or
South Bronx.

You can also use the same handy method for selecting
the name of your new computer software company. Join
the prefix on the left with any suffix on the right:

Data	com
Power	net
Micro	link
Digi	soft
Fibre	logic
Trans	scape

Hence you come up with a perfectly useful name like Datanet, Microlink, Digicom, Fibrescape, or Transnet—all symbolic of a smartly aggressive technologies company.

You can play big-testosterone Hollywood producer with a three-column process that not only names your new summer action movie, but helps you pick a male star for marquee value. Join a word from the first column with any word from the second and any star from the third column:

Brave	*Peace*	Starring Daniel Day-Lewis
Days of	*Hope*	Starring Denzel Washington
Lethal	*Power*	Starring Harrison Ford
Absolute	*Impact*	Starring Mel Gibson
Wild	*Strangers*	Starring Will Smith
Future	*Darkness*	Starring Leslie Nielsen
Tough	*Thunder*	Starring Jackie Chan

Heck, I'd pay $8.50 to see Mel Gibson in *Wild Strangers* or Denzel in *Brave Hope*. I'd pay to see Harrison Ford in anything: *Tough Peace, Lethal Impact, Days of Darkness*.

In the workplace, words so evoke feelings of comfort and familiarity that we even create our own jargon—a shorthand style of communicating within a given profession. Trade jargon also helps us feel like we're part of a community. It serves to identify and separate the insiders from the outsiders.

Horse breeders have geldings, studs, yearlings, foals, Arabs, grays, and sires. The film industry uses jargon like best boy, gaffer, clapper loader, inkydink, pork chop, Foley, and greensman.

There are occupations that for some reason never developed their own jargon and so they adopted the jargon of another trade. Bankers stole their jargon from plumbers: cash flow, dried-up capital, fluid economy, took a bath, down the drain, float a loan, dissolve a partnership, flood the market, laundered money, liquid assets, siphon funds, getting soaked, and frozen assets.

Stand-up comedy borrows its jargon from the language of fighting and civil unrest: he was a riot, she's a scream, you're a crack-up, I got a kick out of him, I bombed. There is slapstick, a gag, a punchline, and finally, such fatal phrases as: I was dyin' out there, You were slayin' 'em, you killed 'em, and you knocked 'em dead.

Then there is the world of business and management whose jargon has become so boring (task-oriented, cross-utilization analysis, synergistic multisourcing, vertical interface, seasonal downsize) that most people prefer to discuss business with jargon stolen from baseball:

I want to *pitch* you a *screwball* idea of mine. If we expect our customers to *play ball* with us, we need to *step up to the plate* with some *big-league* ideas. I'm not *keeping score* here, but lately our *heavy hitters* have been *striking out* with our customers. We always seem to *field* their requests like a bunch of *rookies* and we certainly took our *eyes off the ball* again the last time we had a chance *at bat*. It's my goal to make *major-league fans* out of our customers. I realize that parts of my new business plan will be a *hit,* and parts won't even make it to *first base,* but as long as we can continue to *spitball* new ideas, then I think we'll be able to *play hardball* with the competition and *score big* with our customers. I'd like to *touch base* with you on my new *game plan* for our product *lineup*. I hope you don't *balk* at it because I think it's a real *home run*.

2

THE

PASSION

If you ask me what I came to do in this world, I, an artist, I will answer you: I am here to live out loud.

—ÉMILE ZOLA

Nature's Creative Mechanism

When I was in kindergarten, my personal brand of creativity centered around gluing colorful macaroni to my dad's cigar boxes. When I started growing older I began to learn more about creativity. First I learned about poster paints, paste, and blunt-nose scissors. I learned that you could make paste from flour and water, and make a snowflake by cutting notches in a piece of folded paper. Then one day I started learning how seeds sprout, how birds lay eggs, and how bees pollinate—nature's creativity. It gave me a funny feeling.

You probably started feeling those funny feelings like I did around the age of thirteen when you first saw someone like John Travolta or Joey Heatherton. I took particular notice of my dental assistant, Miss Welch, wearing lipstick and a push-up bra as she x-rayed my bicuspids. No more macaroni and cigar boxes for me! I had discovered nature's creative drive, and I visited the dentist more frequently than any other kid just to get a renewed glimpse at Miss Welch.

Now I feel eminently qualified, being a cartoon producer and all, to comment on most aspects of human sexuality so I can tell you with some certainty that nature's creative process can be easily divided into five parts.

Step 1. The Spark (also the glint, gleam, or that frisky feeling)
Step 2. Conception (you figure it out)
Step 3. Gestation (months of anticipation, worry, and nest building)
Step 4. Birth (painful but exciting)
Step 5. Twenty Years of Grief (raising the baby, also painful but exciting)

The same process works for the lesser animals except it involves considerably more bobbing of heads and showing of plumage and animals forgo the twenty-years-of-grief part, opting instead to kick their young out of the nest or in some cases to eat them. This creation thing also works well for plants: find a fertile patch of soil, plant a seed, water, tend, and voilà—rhubarb.

Astonishing Results

When I was sixteen, things started changing big-time. I became acutely aware that I was not a kid anymore. I could care less about paste and blunt-nose scissors. My voice became lower by the minute, and although I didn't sprout a full beard by lunch like Toad, I did have to shave every third or fourth day! It was about that time that I started to notice the four basic siren calls of a teenage boy's life: cars, girls, alcohol, and really loud music on the radio. (Although I can't be certain, it seemed that the siren calls for girls were a bit different. I think it was something like: makeup, clothes, hair, and topical conversation, but I can't recall.)

I answered my first siren call by buying a 1967 Ford Galaxie 500. I don't know what the "500" meant but it sounded big, like the Indianapolis 500. It sounded loud and dangerous. It sounded like men. Nothing is linked more directly to a man's ego than his car. It is a two-thousand-pound, shiny, quivering steel symbol of everything he stands for. I don't think girls had the same feelings about their cars. They seemed to think of them as a form of, get this, transportation.

For men a car is a gas-burning Pegasus, anxiously chomping at the bit to fly us away to Olympian boulevards yet unexplored. Since we are easily distracted by chrome, men seem to attach themselves to major appliances in a way that women would never dream of. It starts in puberty when we men will, as the Scriptures exhort us to, "leave our mothers and cleave to our car, boat, and big-screen television."

A few years ago I went out looking for a big-screen

TV. I had lived quite happily with a nineteen-inch television set for years but felt the pressure that all American
males feel when the other guys at the office increase the
size of their TVs. Most everyone else had at least a thirty-
two-inch screen at home and one of my best friends had
just purchased a mind-numbing fifty-inch big-screen
model. Wow, fifty inches! My impressionable middle-aged
head wandered into a glassy-eyed rhapsodic state as I suddenly flashed back to my seminal big-screen experience at
the Rosecrans Drive-in. I shook it off and left immediately
for the appliance store.

Mine was the kind of electronics superstore that was
populated by smiling squadrons of commission-seeking
salesmen in crisp white shirts and red ties. In the television
department there must have been a hundred television sets
large and small, all tuned to a Denver Broncos football
game. It was an amazing sight. There were a hundred John
Elways fading back to pass a hundred footballs. The commercials featured a hundred cans of Bud Light being bran-
dished by a hundred incredibly parched-but-handsome
men. The big-screen television sets sat on the floor in the
middle of the department. On a fifty-inch set, John Elway
was huge. His helmet was the size of a bison and the
surround-sound system would have liquefied my spine
had I stood any closer. These big-screen models ooze tes-
tosterone. I noticed that I was sprouting a full beard just
by being in the vicinity of one.

A salesman wandered up and asked if I would like to
try one out. "Sure," I said confidently, sounding as though
I had just been asked to test drive a Bugatti. There were
no controls on the big-screen itself so the salesman used
the remote to surf past CNN, Tiny Toons, and PGA golf.
The picture came to rest on some sort of infomercial as

the television salesman began telling me about some of the television's other features. He waxed on about some electronic thing but his spiel ground to a halt as we both noticed what the infomercial was about. There on the screen was what appeared to be an enlightened woman who was selling audio tapes about how to have a better sex life at home. She was fielding tough, unbiased questions from a tough, unbiased host in a tough, unbiased Armani suit who was hired to ask her stumpers like, "What exactly is it that men are looking for in bed?"

The lady always seemed to have the answers to his questions, and in a well-prepared spontaneous response she would articulate with great enthusiasm and in vivid detail the particulars of what men wanted in bed. And I thought I had an interesting job.

After each answer, the tough unbiased host would sit on the edge of his seat, furrow his brow and reply "interesting"—damn right it's interesting. If there is one thing that can attract the attention of a group of people in an electronics store, it's an infomercial on human sexuality.

Infomercials are like car crashes for me, they're horrible but I can't look away. And by the look of it neither could the studio audience, who seemed to sit on the edge of their seats with that paid-to-look-interested expression.

Now all I really wanted to do that morning was to buy a television, so I did my best to tune out the infomercial and listened intently to the salesman as he gathered his thoughts and continued to tell me about all the features of this television set. In doing so he began to crank up the volume to demonstrate the stereo speakers. The volume slowly swelled to its loudest point, eclipsing even the roar of 60,000 Bronco fans cheering on one hundred television sets, and just as it reached unbearable levels, the lady on the infomercial said, ". . . and sometimes all the man wants to do is caress her buttocks." Every head in the store turned and looked at us. It's not every day you hear the word *buttocks* spoken so loudly that it would drown out the roar of a Blue Angels flyby.

Just then the telephone rang and the salesman left to answer it. I was left standing alone in front of what now seemed like the biggest and loudest television set in the northern hemisphere. I went to turn down the volume but the salesman had taken the remote control with him. The other people in the store looked on with disgusted interest as I stood there alone, three feet from the screen where the host began questioning a couple who had used these audio cassettes, "and with astonishing results." (I don't know about you, but I rarely associate astonishing results in the bedroom with an audio cassette unless it involves Frank Sinatra.)

By now a small crowd had gathered, wondering who I was and why was I not watching the Broncos like everyone else. Aside from this uncomfortable situation, this was of course one of those mornings when I didn't feel like showering and I just ran out the door wearing ripped shorts, filthy old tennis shoes, bad hair, and a T-shirt emblazoned with I'M A PEPPER!

The salesman returned and I asked him, through politely clenched teeth, to turn down the volume a little bit, which he did only after slowly and meticulously showing me how all of the color and tint adjustments worked. The infomercial came to a climax with glowing testimonials by grinning squadrons of young married couples who had obviously done exactly what the tapes recommended and once again experienced "astonishing results." I decided that nineteen inches was big enough for my televiewing needs and excused myself from the showroom, trying to avoid eye contact with anyone.

I noticed something that day. Everyone in my electronics store seemed interested in sex. And since the demographics of my electronics store are statistically aligned with the demographics of the entire planet, I can only deduce that all people are interested in sex. Sure, there may be profound differences in the siren calls of the sexes, but the relationship between man and woman and the reproductive act itself represents nature's creative and rejuvenative mechanism and that's why we're so interested.

We make babies, then we make homes for them, clothes for them, cartoons for them. And the same curiosity and passion that drive our sexual fascination seem akin to the curiosity and passion that drive the creative spirit. Some experts even say we sublimate our sexual desires and translate them into our creative passions. Our desire to reproduce is perhaps the most fundamental expression of our desire to create.

Expressions

Growing from an adolescent to a teen to an adult makes for big changes in life. Once upon a time we would play hard from morning to night and our brain grew exponentially with each connection, each stimulation. As children we were willing to sing, dance, and sneak into bed with a colander in our pants, but now as adults, day by day, little by little we start to edit ourselves. We fear embarrassment. We try to decide what career paths to follow. We want to be adults, and so our play turns slowly to work. We forsake toys and teddy bears for basics like food, shelter, and the Abdominizer for washboard abs in sixty days or less. But even the lowest animals seek these basic things (except for the washboard abs part). Remember again that we are separated from the animal kingdom not because of our opposable thumb and hairless body. We are different not only because we eat sitting down or because we have a predisposition to enter the Publishers Clearing House Sweepstakes. We are different because we create. We create beyond the fundamentals of food, clothing, and shelter and into the soaring and spiritually enriching arenas of music, fashion, art, and architecture. We create because we have to. It's what we do. Every day our senses bombard us with a spectrum of impressions. These impressions imprint powerfully on our souls. We can keep these impressions inside where they can build up and clog our drain or we can spill them out in wonderful flowing expressions of how we interpret life.

We are meant to express how we feel about life. It's like breathing: Inhale the experiences of life, exhale how you feel about them. We are at our best when we can turn our impressions into expressions. The equation goes like this: impression without expression equals depression.

We tend to express ourselves in natural and uninhibited ways. Our human creative pattern flows naturally and in much the same way as nature's creative process flows: from spark to conception, to gestation, to birth. The natural process of creation happens constantly. All around us trees and animals and mountain ranges spring up from the chaotic soil of earth. Creation is not just some distant prehistoric event that God accomplished in seven days, but rather a ubiquitous constant that surrounds us every day of our lives. We live in the midst of constant creation.

We are instinctively creative just as the world around us is inherently creative. But sometimes as our thoughts become more sophisticated, we try to intellectualize and study the creative process—a process that we used to do instinctively. The creative process has been written about and dissected for many years and not so surprisingly, the textbook description of the creative process is often patterned on nature:

Step 1. The Idea (same as the Spark)
Step 2. Immersion (similar to Conception, but not as much fun)
Step 3. Incubation (Gestation without the morning sickness)
Step 4. The "Eureka" Moment (the Birth)
Step 5. Verification (the Twenty-Years-of-Grief part)

It's important not to take these steps too seriously. We create a million times a day without thinking about it and we frequently create in ways that don't fall into a five-step process.

Here's another way of looking at the creative process that lists nine things you might feel when you are grappling with a problem. It's not that every time we bake some cookies we rigidly go through each of these nine steps, but when we are trying to innovate or come up with a new perspective, we'll probably cross paths with most of them.

Creation is a very personal, nonlinear process. In other words, it doesn't happen in a straight line and no two people do it alike. I include these steps not so you might study them and try to check them off like some grocery list. I include them to validate them—to say that it's okay to travel down these sideroads during your creative journey. See if any of these sound familiar to you:

Anticipation—hunting
Preparation—gathering
Hesitation—the fear
Frustration—dead ends, roadblocks, and potholes
Constipation—full of information and anxiety but no
   breakthrough
Improvisation—try all the possibilities
Immersion—time to think, time to absorb
Inspiration—the birth of a solution . . . eureka, creativity!
Perspiration—the hard work of discovery

Anticipation

From some mysterious ethos comes a germ of an idea. It might come in the guise of a goal: "I want to write an opera" or "I want to make a curry," or it might come in the form of a question: "What would happen if I dropped this rubber on the stovetop?" It might even begin with a siren call of possibility. A blank piece of paper, a dinner plate, or an empty parcel of land can call us to action simply because they represent boundless possibility and are a waiting receptacle for our imagination.

Just like a skydiver, the defining moment in writing, cooking, architecture, or dance is when you decide to leave the safety of inaction and leap into the unknown void. The courage and willingness to jump into that void and feel the rush of the wind in the hope that you will be able to spread your wings and fly . . . that is the touchstone of the creative process. We've got an idea and we are flush with anticipation. Our mind races with the possibilities. We leap.

Preparation

Preparation assumes an intellectual preparation: an openness to all possibilities regardless of how far-fetched or contradictory they may be to your present knowledge and belief. It also assumes an emotional and physical preparation: a taking stock of yourself to know where your strengths and vulnerabilities lie. To prepare is to be like a sponge ready to absorb.

Our emotions are fed from endless sources. Part of your preparation for a creative journey is to seek out those sources and open yourself to their gift of inspiration. Picasso said:

> The artist is a receptacle for emotions that come from all over the place: from the sky, from the earth, from a scrap of paper, from a passing shape, from a spider's web. That is why we must not discriminate between things. Where things are concerned there are no class distinctions. We must pick out what is good for us where we can find it—except from our own works. I have a horror of copying myself, but when I am shown a portfolio of old drawings, for instance, I have no qualms about taking anything I want from them.

We prepare by reading books and watching films, we prepare by studying manuscripts and visiting galleries. There is another kind of preparation that Picasso alludes to. We prepare by being open to influences of all kinds. In that way a spider's web or a scrap of paper can be equally as inspirational as a Degas drawing or a quote from Voltaire. We prepare not only by studying within the bounds of our craft, but by searching everywhere for a broad base of inspiration. It's a sort of creative cross-pollination. In his lectures at Harvard, Leonard Bernstein used the evolution of spoken language to help understand the evolution of modern musical harmonies. Marcel Proust used the memories of food to inspire vivid literary pictures of his youth. Frank Lloyd Wright used inspiration from Japanese art to influence his work.

I like the football team that prepares for the season with ballet classes. I like the painter who listens to Miles Davis before she paints. I like the architect who hang glides in order to understand space. Music inspires dance. Dance inspires sculpture. Sculpture inspires architecture. Architecture inspires business. Business inspires mathematics. Mathematics inspires science. Science inspires theology. Theology inspires singing. Singing inspires poetry. Poetry inspires painting and on and on and on.

Hesitation

Hesitation is a very strong and dominant human reaction. It probably stems from the days when we wore animal pelts, carried clubs, and had to decide in a split second what to do when suddenly faced with an angry bear the size of a bus. Hesitation was a method of survival that gave us a brief moment when we could choose to fight the bear and risk death or run from the bear and risk death. This fight or flight reaction—this moment of hesitation when we decide whether to run away or stay and attack—is still working well in modern times and comes in handy when facing an assailant such as a burglar, a mugger, or a mime.

The fight or flight response also comes in handy when facing the creative process. It helps us get a very gut-level assessment for our work. Is an idea worth fighting for or should I just walk away? Do I really want to do this thing? Will I be a hero or a wiener?

Frustration

Most of my lessons in frustration have their roots in the football seasons at Bellflower High. It wasn't easy to play football for a team with a sweet and charming name like Bellflower. Our school was known for scholastic achievement, an excellent auto shop, and hometown hospitality, but not really for football. The team was named the Bellflower Buccaneers in the hope that the buccaneer in us would prevail. It didn't. We were regularly trounced by bigger schools with more ominous-sounding names like Jordan, Downey, Paramount, and Excelsior. Our mascot was a big surly pirate with a big leering buccaneer smile that was meant to look mean and nasty but instead came off looking a little sheepish.

Our pansy-sounding name and reputation put us at the bottom of the football food chain with the exception of St. John Bosco which we regularly punished with our pent-up anger. After the game we felt badly that we took our wrath out on poor St. John Bosco.

I was a drummer in the band and my job at football games was simple . . . pep. Most of the time we dispensed pep in the form of peppy fight songs and cheers during the game. We played for the pep squad so that there would be plenty of pep when the players entered the field, and at the end of each quarter we really let down our hair with such pep-inducing crowd pleasers as "Louie Louie" and the theme from *Hawaii Five-O*.

When it was almost halftime, the band would line up on the sidelines while the teams ran their last few plays. The quarterback waited until the band was lined up on the sidelines and then called a special crowd-pleasing play that sent the entire team rushing at full sprint into the saxophone section. It was quite a sight.

When the horn sounded at the end of the first half, the team ran to the locker room and the fans ran to the refreshment stand, leaving the band nearly alone in the stadium to start the halftime festivities.

Our announcer was usually a senior whose prematurely active hormones had endowed him with a deep FM-radio announcer voice. He would begin: . . . "Ladies and gentlemen, please welcome the mighty Bellflower marching Buccaneer Band." Having a well-composed halftime show required a theme like "A Salute to Broadway" or "A Salute to the Irish" or "A Salute to Sonny and Cher." The tricky thing was to come up with formations for each song. Some were more successful than others, for example, you could always get a hand for forming a Mississippi river boat with a turning paddle wheel and playing "When the Saints Go Marchin' In." For extra credit, we would borrow the fire extinguisher from the band room and shoot smoke out the top of the smoke stacks. Now that's a crowd pleaser.

One time we formed a top hat, gloves, and cane and played "Puttin' on the Ritz" to the concerted yawns of the crowd, which couldn't figure out what we were forming except that it was vaguely reminiscent of a giant squid. Another time for our Irish show, we formed two huge circles with a tuba player in the center of each and played "When Irish Eyes Are Smiling." It was supposed to be a set of giant eyes until an imaginative student shouted from the snack bar, "Looks like tits!" In retrospect we should have formed a shamrock. It was all very frustrating.

Entertaining a crowd at a football game took on a new dimension the next year with the addition of the dance squad. Everyone loved the dance squad. Just the term *dance squad* fascinated me. I imagined them being some sort of tactical squad that would break into boring situations and perform emergency dance routines on request.

A typical halftime show went like this: We'd march onto the field playing a crowd pleaser like "Smoke on the Water" followed by some patriotic tune like "The Battle Hymn of the Republic" (we learned early that people enjoy a little flag waving with their football). Then we'd line up in concertlike formation in front of the stands and out would come the dance squad wearing nothing more than leotards and big hair. Then we'd play a James Brown hit like "I Feel Good" and the dance squad would dance and the crowd would go crazy. Then we'd play some Broadway tune like the theme from *Oklahoma!* while forming what appeared to be a giant saucepan but was meant to be the map of Oklahoma. This is when most of the fans would either go to the bathroom or yell, "Why are you standing there forming a giant saucepan? Bring back the dance squad."

We would finish by forming a giant B for Bellflower and we'd play the Buccaneer fight song, "Onward Bellflower" (which sounded strangely like "On Wisconsin"). We had the crowd in the palm of our hand. They sang, they stomped, they cheered, and when it was over we returned to the stands with a renewed sense of accomplishment.

It took many frustrating games to find the right combination of elements that made the entire fifteen minutes of halftime festivities a scintillating piece of visual and au- ral entertainment. I don't think we ever got better at foot- ball, but the rules for successful halftime entertainment were set in my impressionable head for life. Have a theme. Open with a big number. Always have a dance squad. Cut the bathroom break song. End with a rousing fight song.

Constipation

Here is a very delicate but important subject. Sometimes during the creative process we take in loads and loads of information and inspiration and seem ready to explode, but nothing happens. The idea that all of this preparation yields nothing can be incredibly frustrating, not to mention uncomfortable. Creativity is a process of sometimes long periods of incubation. The ideas don't always flow smoothly and at times even hard work and desire won't spur a creative breakthrough. Recognizing this sort of cre- ative backup is important. Your head probably won't ex- plode if an idea doesn't emerge, but it's crucial to have the faith that one day a breakthrough will most certainly come. It's so easy to give up at this stage and walk away from your problem, but it's more important to dominate your ideas than let your ideas dominate you. You need to hang in there and keep trying.

There was a scene in *The Lion King* that wasn't working very well. It's a scene where adult Simba returns secretly to Pride Rock with Nala, Pumbaa, and Timon. Simba tries to talk Timon and Pumbaa into creating a diversion.

The scene started with Simba asking his buddies to cre- ate a diversion. In an early version, Timon and Pumbaa did a vaudevillelike soft-shoe routine and bantered back and forth:

> TIMON: Hey Pumbaa, it looks like you've put on a few pounds.
> PUMBAA: Yep, boy, I ate like a pig.
> TIMON: Why, you look like you could feed a family of four.
> Et cetera.

The scene was a smile but not a laugh and we needed a big laugh at that point in the movie. It was the last chance for some shtick before we launched into a very dramatic third act.

So late one night the directors, writers, and I were holding three pizzas hostage in our tomblike story room, trying to find a better gag. About an hour later, we had consumed enough pizza to feed the entire population of Saddleback Peak Estates. We had done nothing particularly creative with our time, save for the little happy face we had made with pineapples and olives on the last remaining slice. We were all incredibly constipated (and here I speak metaphorically even though we had each consumed a metric ton of cheese). We stared blankly at the last happy slice of pizza and hoped it would speak to us. We couldn't come up with a good idea.

"What if Timon has a cowboy hat on and Pumbaa's on a barbecue."

Silence. We stared at the pizza but it offered no wisdom.

"What if there's this big banquet table and . . . naw . . . oh, how about a backyard barbecue and Timon could wear a big chef's hat and an apron that says KISS THE COOK."

More silence.

Then in a moment of divine intervention the pizza finally spoke. It shouted: "Hey, how about a luau!" We all laughed a crazy what-a-stupid-idea laugh when the directors stopped and said, "Hey, how about a luau?"

We could do a luau with Pumbaa as the suckling pig and Timon as the hula-dancing pitch man. We cobbled together some lyrics for a hula, then grabbed an empty five-gallon water bottle for a drum and an animator who had a ukulele in his room (more common than you would think) to try out the song.

> If you're hungry for a hunk of fat and juicy meat
> Eat my buddy Pumbaa here because he is a treat.
> Come on and dine, on this tasty swine.
> All you gotta do is get in line
> Are you achin'
> For some bacon?
> He's a big pig, you can be a big pig, too. Hey!

It ain't Shakespere but it made us laugh. The next week we recorded Nathan Lane singing the song. He also recorded the lines that led into the song, which went something like this:

> TIMON: How we gonna distract these guys?
> SIMBA: Live bait.
> TIMON: Great idea! (*a beat of realization*) Hey!
> SIMBA: Come on Timon, you guys have to create a diversion.
> TIMON: What do you want me to do, wear a skirt and do the hula?

About five takes later, Nathan got bored with the last line and blurted out, "What do you want me to do, dress in drag and do the hula?" Luckily the tape was still running and we knew we had a scene.

Timon would say this line and we'd cut ahead in time to him wearing a grass skirt and singing about his delicious buddy Pumbaa. We wanted to use the melody to the old Hawaiian war chant. The music attorney had warned us that it would cost a lot since the melody was owned by another music publisher. It had better be one big gut buster for it to be worth the cost. We still wanted to try it at the next preview screening.

When the big night came, we gathered in the lobby of a nearby theater and watched as the audience filed in. Our fate was in their hands. It must be what it feels like to be a defendant and watch the jury take their seats, except the legal system discourages popcorn and nachos in the jury box. We had refined the movie in many spots, added laughs, and cut our fat, but the biggest question of the evening was: Will the luau gag work?

The lights went down and we took our seats in the back of the auditorium. The movie played really well and as we approached the time for the luau gag, my stomach sank. Were we nuts? What's so funny about a meerkat in a grass skirt? When it came time I closed my eyes and wrapped my hand around the cup holder in my seat as though I was on a catapult about to be launched into the screen at high speed if the gag didn't work. Timon said his "dress in drag" line, and the laughter drowned out most of the lyrics to the hula song. We had our big laugh and I could unpeel my fingers from my seat, all because of some cold pizza, desperation, constipation, and, eventually, inspiration.

Improvisation

Improvisation is something we normally associate with jazz musicians. Musicians take a line of melody, spin it around, and turn it into their own. Great cooks improvise, great writers improvise, dancers, lawyers, actors, magicians, and painters all improvise.

Picasso said: "A picture is not thought out and settled beforehand. While it is being done it changes as one's thoughts change. And when it is finished, it still goes on changing, according to the state of mind of whoever is looking at it. A picture lives a life like a living creature, undergoing the changes imposed on us by our life from day to day. This is natural enough, as the picture lives only through the man who is looking at it."

So next time you set out to paint a landscape with a bunch of trees, and you follow the mobility of your thoughts and end up painting a portrait of the Hawaiian Tropics Bikini Team, realize that improvisation is at play.

Improvisation shouldn't be completely foreign to us. We improvise constantly in our everyday life. We'll start out to do some errands and halfway there our thoughts will change and we decide to stop for coffee. When we get back in the car we remember to buy stamps and stop at the pet store to look at the puppies. We wouldn't think twice about having the freedom to change our plans when we go out to buy groceries, why wouldn't we welcome the same freedom when we create? You'll still arrive at the grocery store, and even if you don't it probably means that it wasn't important to go there in the first place.

All projects change in the course of their journey. It's best to start with a plan and then expect accidents along the way—accidents that allow you to revise the plan, "plus" the plan, and make it far better than when the journey began. Creativity demands that we be spontaneous enough to follow the merit of a better idea. Planning for spontaneity and improvisation can be tricky. It's hard to budget and schedule for a creative process that allows ideas to surface at any time, even late in the game, yet that's exactly what businesses need for innovation. The entire team from the top to the trenches needs to improvise together.

This may seem chancy and accidental. It may even seem lazy or irresponsible, but those "accidents" are the stuff of innovation. Those improvisations allow us to explore new areas of our work. They encourage us to stop repeating ourselves and to reach out and explore new ideas. How we deal with accidents reveals much more about us than how we deal with plans.

There was a day on *The Lion King* when Hans Zimmer had done a stirring arrangement of "The Circle of Life" in preparation for a singer to come in and record the vocals . . . but something was missing. We knew that to establish the African setting, we wanted a more indigenous sound from the first note of the film. Hans invited African singer Lebo M. to the studio to try some experiments on tape. At the time, Hans worked in an improvised space that he had carved out of the back of a nondescript industrial building on Santa Monica Boulevard.

The inside of the studio didn't even have a glass partition to separate the recording booth from the area where the talent stood at the microphone. The room was stacked with boxes of tapes, old guitars, a piano, and a table laden with Chinese food in the corner. It was in that back-room studio where Lebo put down his egg roll, stepped up to the microphone, and began recording. He experimented a few times to find something unique—a sort of tribal cry—and then on the next take, out of nowhere, came the now famous cry in the wilderness that begins *The Lion King*. It was improvised quickly, crudely, and with very little preparation, but it worked. It captured the mood of an entire film.

Singer Carmen Twilly came to the studio that night to sing the vocal track for "The Circle of Life." By late that evening the crew had finished up all the moo shu shrimp, bang bang chicken, and kung pao pork and Carmen had finished recording an extraordinary version of the whole song. At the time, Carmen's performance was meant to be a demo or temporary vocal which would eventually be discarded and replaced. For months we listened to other singers, looking for a permanent vocalist for "The Circle of Life," but in the end we could never improve on Carmen's emotional delivery, recorded that night in a backroom studio on Santa Monica Boulevard. The setting was improvised—part recording studio, part store room, part Chinese bistro—but the work was fresh and soulful.

Immersion

Richard Williams is one of the most creative people I know. He carved out his career-making television commercials in London for twenty years while all the while working through the night on his dream, an animated film called *The Thief*. The commercials weren't his creative outlet, although they were full of ingenuity and brilliance. Dick wanted to make a film and for twenty years *The Thief* consumed him.

Dick worked on his film in a most interesting way. Little sequences of film would emerge based on a character or a part of a story. He'd see a movie and become inspired, run home, and animate. The film progressed for years in this mosaic fashion.

The other thing Dick did was teach. In the prime of his career, he went to the cinema and saw Disney's *Jungle Book*, and upon leaving the theater proclaimed three words that every middle-aged man dreads: I know nothing. (There are lots of three-word phrases that middle-aged men dread: Change the diapers, Lose some weight, Dry the dishes, No football today. This is the all-encompassing fear, the confirmation that all your life you've been an impostor.)

Dick didn't collapse with this realization. He set about with a relentless drive to learn. He found all of the surviving animators who worked with Walt Disney or at Warner Bros. or MGM during the golden age of animation. He'd fly them to London for classes, or when they wouldn't come he'd send them sequences of *The Thief* to work on. Then when they'd turn in their artwork, he'd study it and play it for himself and his close-knit team of animators.

I worked with Dick for two years on *Who Framed Roger Rabbit*. After spending a few weeks with him in the studio, it shocked me that this legend of animation seemed to do very little work. He'd come in in the morning and we'd talk a while. Then he'd take a call. Then when faced with a deadline for designing Jessica Rabbit, instead of sitting at a desk and pulling out a pencil, he left the studio. About an hour later, he came back from the bookstore with loads of magazines and books under his arm and proceeded to pull out a scissors and cut up the books. Each clipping was an idea. That girl's hair, this one's eyes, that actress's body, her dress. Dozens of clippings were snipped from books, magazines, and posters and then Dick would tape them to big white cards. I'd ask to help, but he'd always say, "No, no, it's this thing I do, and I really have to do it."

I thought he was nuts. Why are we paying this director to cut out pictures and tape them to a board? But as eccentric as Dick was, he was smart. Really smart. He knew about immersion. He went on for weeks with this clipping and pasting routine. When he wasn't clipping, he was taking home cartoons and watching them until the early hours of the morning. When he wasn't watching cartoons, he'd go out for coffee with Roy.

Roy Naisbett was a master designer and special effects artist who made his career working on Stanley Kubrick's *2001: A Space Odyssey*. But Roy and Dick didn't talk about movies when they went out. They'd order double eggs on toast with coffee and they'd talk. They'd talk about politics, talk about the studio, talk about the food, and talk about Dick's favorite cornet player Bix Beiderbecke. After the bill was paid, and just before they got up, Dick would invariably say, ". . . Oh, oh I had this idea for a shot." They'd sit down again and with a borrowed pen and a napkin, Dick would sketch a few postage-stamp-size drawings—scribbles that were the genesis of a brilliant idea.

Then there were Sundays at the Grosvenor House Hotel. Dick played the cornet and loved jazz. Every Sunday, he'd roll out of bed and grab his horn and take a cab to Grosvenor Square where he played with an unlikely group of musician friends called Dick's Six. On Sundays the Grosvenor House had a buffet brunch which, as far as I could tell, featured only salads that could be made with bulk mayonnaise. There were peas and mayonnaise, carrots and mayonnaise, corn, cheese, and beets with mayonnaise. In the middle of the buffet, there would be a hot beef dish, some chicken, some fish, some lettuce, and then in big crocks at the end of the buffet, more mayonnaise.

The Sunday brunch lured mainly tourists and hotel guests who had come to eat their fill at the buffet, drink free champagne, and listen to the jazz. And what glorious jazz it was. At break times, the band would huddle in a back corner near the kitchen to laugh and talk about Dick, the Knicks, chicks, Bix, and politics. As far as I could tell it was the only place on the planet where you could watch an animator play the cornet and consume a kilo of mayonnaise all for one low price. Once in a while, Dick would invite me to play drums for a set. It was better than the pep band. It was heaven.

The point I finally understood after dealing with Dick's free spirit, and the manic "Where's Dick?" calls from the studio, was that this was his process. This was every bit as valid a process as any artist's. The clippings, the double eggs on toast, the cornet, the mayonnaise were all somehow linked. Dick drank up a big diet of inspiration from every imaginable source, and then, often in the middle of the night, he would hover over his drawing table where the drawings would leap like fire out of the ends of his fingers and onto the paper. His weeks of immersion, of idea gathering, would come out in heaping torrents of nonstop work. The deadline was here. The work got finished at an alarming rate. It was all brilliant.

Inspiration

The moment of inspiration is magical. The moment when all of the input and research and frustration combines to create a spark, a breakthrough, a solution—the Eureka Moment.

This spark of inspiration can come quietly in the dead of night to a writer hunched over his keyboard. Or it can feel like a skyrocket when an idea emerges from a collaborative group of people. Both are valid. Both are inexplicable gifts. We need only to learn how to recognize and act on an inspiration and not discount it because it is our own. Read carefully what Ralph Waldo Emerson said about trusting your own inspirations and the consequences of ignoring them:

> A man should learn to detect and watch that gleam of light which flashes across his mind from within, . . . yet he dismisses without notice his thought, because it is his. In every work of genius we recognize our own rejected thoughts; they come back to us with a certain alienated majesty. Great works of art have no more affecting lesson for us than this. They teach us to abide by our spontaneous impression with more good-humored inflexibility than most when the whole cry of voices is on the other side. Else tomorrow a stranger will say with masterly good sense precisely what we have thought and felt all the time, and we shall be forced to take with shame our own opinion from another.
>
> —RALPH WALDO EMERSON, *SELF-RELIANCE*, 1841

Perspiration

Tom appeared on the sidewalk with a bucket of whitewash and a long-handled brush. He surveyed the fence, and all gladness left him and a deep melancholy settled down upon his spirit. Thirty yards of board fence nine feet high, life to him seemed hollow, and existence but a burden.

—MARK TWAIN

One of the elements that unifies the lives of extremely creative people is their capacity for hard work. People who are consistently creating seem driven by some unseen force. They are absorbed in their work and will put in almost any number of hours to reach a breakthrough.

Hard work doesn't guarantee anything will happen, it simply gives you better odds. If you had a crystal ball that said you would have a life-changing success but first you would have a hundred failures, wouldn't you want to get to work and get those hundred failures out of the way? Work moves us through the process with purpose and regularity. You must foster the habit of going to work on a project even if you feel tired or blocked. If you had to wait until you felt inspired and fresh before you sat down to work, you wouldn't get too far.

Some work is physical in nature. Throwing a pot, or sculpting, or spending long hours on your feet in front of an easel engages your body in the act of creation. This demanding physical involvement in your work may even be the essence of your creative expression as it is with dancers and actors. Even painters, cooks, and musicians bring a physical vitality to their work. A painting, after all, is a sort of record of the painter's gestures. In a good restaurant you can feel the kinetic energy coming from the kitchen, a violinist weaves and sways during a performance charging a piece of music with tremendous physical life.

Other forms of creation are more intellectual in nature. The writer, the poet, the architect must conduct their work in thought and contemplation. But even here, the proceeds of their thoughts must evoke a physical reaction within us. Great writers and poets make us feel like we are with them on their journey. We can believe and relate to their characters and feel like we share their problems. The intellectual ideas of great architects are made manifest with the use of space, color, texture, and acoustics. We enter a building and feel awe, wonder, respect, charm, comfort, or stability.

To work at a painting implies that we dash to our easel, pick up a brush, and paint until we drop, but the mental work we do is more crucial to finishing our painting than just the sweat equity we invest in it. Sometimes we need to solve problems first before we approach the canvas. There are musicians who close their eyes and imagine their performance, doing most of their practicing without their instrument in hand. Writers take long walks and do a mountain of mental work before they approach the typewriter. There are composers who would never dream of sitting at a piano when they write music, but prefer to write in their mind first. Filmmakers see their movie on an imaginary screen in their head long before it goes to the multiplex.

The physical act of working with paint, canvas, brushes, keyboards, or movie cameras is all craft and can be learned to a degree. The mental engine that drives the craft is what makes you a unique human being. The way in which you work both your physical craft and your mental engine will drive your creative accomplishments. We are most likely to fail when we focus too much on one or the other; we are most likely to feel satisfied if we work to balance the mental and physical self.

Work doesn't end when the project is over. Even then, artists must have the tenacity of spirit to test their work, to show their work and to communicate their work to the world. It takes persistence to give birth to a new idea. It takes work to turn an idea into a tangible expression of yourself. It takes work and tact to bring an innovation to the movie screen, the art gallery, the stage, or the market-place.

Good-bye Surf and Turf

Now we have some sense of the creative processes at play in our lives. This frustration-laden process is useful if we are faced with the task of inventing a solution to a prob-lem. What happens, though, if we have reached some level of success, and then watched our success fade? How can we face the daunting task of reinventing ourselves—with reviving our ideas that were once vibrant but have now grown stale? When faced with these riddles of life, I forgo the advice of the great psychologists of our era and look instead to the food service industry for the answer.

About twenty-five years ago, dining out at a fancy res-taurant would mean the Monday-night steak special at the Sizzler steak house across the street from Bellflower High School. There you could get the complete top sirloin steak dinner, which included baked potatoes and their famous Texas toast (a piece of garlic bread the size of one of those cushions you take to the football game). This became a family tradition except for once in a while when we could talk our dad into international cuisine, which usually con-sisted of the "five-for-a-dollar" chimichanga night at Casa de Pepe.

I was jealous of my older brother and sister who started to go on dates to more chic, grown-up places with names like The Rusty Pelican, Moonshadows, or The Cork and Cleaver. It was here amid the macramé plant hangers,

Captain and Tennille music, and a menu filled with exotic things like mahi mahi and artichokes, that you could find the young man's dream entree, the surf and turf: "a generous cut of prime rib served with fresh New England lobster tail, drawn butter, and a Texas-style baked potato (the size of a small child) smothered in butter and sour cream." And, as if that weren't enough saturated fat, you could have a decadent dessert item with a name that sounded like it came from a pulpit-pounding sermon on fundamentalist sin: devil's food sundae, death by chocolate, Satan's fudge pie, chocolate madness, and lady fingers soaked in rum.

Then a few years ago something changed. Eating out got boring, business sagged as people became more health-conscious, and the industry had to reinvent itself or be doomed to a lifetime of serving liver and onions to blue-haired ladies. Creativity hit the restaurant business in a big way. Out with the surf and turf, the garlic mushroom caps, deep-fried cheese sticks, and the Texas-style anything. In with the shellfish and tiger prawn paella with shrimp-tomato couscous, wild boar bratwurst with horseradish cream and apple walnut chutney, crab falafel salad with saffron pita, red pepper tahini with salsify chips, and sizzling Jamaican chicken sausage on a bed of baby chicory with shiitake mushroom polenta. For a while I wasn't sure that I wanted to eat a baby chicory or for that matter, anything with a name like shiitake. But what these adventuresome chefs were bringing their hungry patrons was not just food as sustenance, but food as experience and entertainment.

It's easy to get seduced into this wonderful world of culinary hyperbole where even a glass of water becomes "eau minerale served chilled with a citrus wedge in a

Welsh crystal cylinder.'' The restaurant industry's blend of
international ingredients, colorful adjectives, and show-
manship has not only brought a lot of fun back to the experience of eating out, but it has also crept into other
industries with interesting results:

- Politics: John Doe, candidate
  for Senate, gentle-minded
  public servant mingled with
  humility, seasoned with
  experience, no ordinary
  Texas-style politician (here,
  I guess Texas-style is a
  negative).
- Music: His flavors of
  Brazilian samba are mixed
  with influences from flamenco
  on a bed of American
  jazz.
- Cars: Rich Corinthian leather
  (I prefer cow leather, but hey,
  I hear rich Corinthians are
  very soft and supple), with
  four tiger-paw steel-belted
  radials and a sizzling-hot
  power train.
- Insurance: The comfort of
  reliable coverage with the
  assurance of a family-run
  business based on pride,
  personal service, and
  integrity.

- Movies: A sizzling blend of white-knuckle action, high-drama thrill ride, and an age-old love story that will turn your stomach and warm your heart.

Macro and Micro

My day today was filled with uncountable acts of creativity. For example, this morning I created a small oil painting, by noon I had an idea for a new movie, and by nightfall I had put a fine wax finish on my car and came up with a new recipe for tangy lamb shank (try to say that five times quickly). All these acts of creativity brought joy to me and my family and so I will continue oil painting and waxing my car for years to come. But will any of these creations change the world as we know it? Well, with the possible exception of my tangy lamb shank recipe . . . no.

Creativity happens in this world on two levels. The micro level of daily creations would include things like my fine car wax job and my tangy lamb shank recipe. The macro level of creativity would include a creation that gets the world to sit up and take notice: the invention of the cell phone (which by all accounts was invented by Hedy Lamarr when she wasn't wearing a thong and playing Tondeleo), a Picasso painting, a Frank Capra movie, a Frank Lloyd Wright building. These macro works and macro artists are embraced by society for their vision. They change us, inspire us, and give us a new perspective on ourselves.

The micro level of creativity has to do with very personal satisfaction and joy. The macro level of creativity suggests an innovation that becomes part of the culture with the potential to change the way we perceive things or the way in which we live. The hardest thing for many people to understand is that both have validity.

The small painting you do for your mom can have a more profound effect on her life than some dusty masterpiece hanging in a museum. Cultures need the macro masterstrokes of creativity in order to evolve. Things like the invention of the microchip, the motion picture camera, or the refrigerator brought about global revolutions in thought and in the quality of life.

The human race has embraced many great artistic masterworks and celebrated stunning scientific innovation, but thrives on more than that. We thrive on the thousands of small meaningful and intensely personal innovations that the people close to us produce every day. The hand-knit sweater, the specially baked pie, the love letter. These micro works won't revolutionize the progress of the human race. They do, however, make important and lasting connections in our lives—personal connections to people close to us via their creative gifts. The breathtaking cultural change brought on by acts of macro creativity and the intimate personal connections brought on by acts of micro creativity are both crucially important to the quality of our lives.

All for One

The meeting of two personalities is like the contact of two chemical substances: if there is any reaction, both are transformed.

—CARL GUSTAV JUNG

Creativity is seldom a solo act. No one ever creates alone in a vacuum. We are hopelessly social creatures—hunter-gatherers—who collect our nuts and berries of knowledge from one another and then spit them out in new and interesting ways. It's true that some are better at the process than others, some excel at their craft, some work harder, and some are better at self-promotion than others. But in the sea of creativity, no one is an island. No one is truly an original. All individual accomplishment stands on the shoulders of those who have come before.

In her book *Writing Down the Bones*, author Natalie Goldberg talks about a writer's fears of being unoriginal: "We always worry that we are copying someone else, that we don't have our own style. Don't worry. Writing is a communal act. Contrary to popular belief, a writer is not Prometheus alone on a hill full of fire. We are very arrogant to think we alone have a totally original mind. We are carried on the backs of all the writers who came before us."

If we are so dependent on others for our creative input, why then do we want to sneak off to a cottage in the mountains to write a novel in solitude? The collection of research and inspiration for our novel can be and should be a very communal thing. We talk and study and listen and debate and eat and fill our intellectual tummies to excess. The regurgitation—the creative outpouring, if you will—is very personal. The brain needs quiet time to put together the many abstract pieces of its collective experience into a usable, interesting, and hopefully new form.

Over time our thoughts fall into predictable habits, so it's not only natural, but helpful when we escape our familiar surroundings in search of a new environment that will inspire us. Our brain is jolted out of its comfort zone with new sensory experiences. When we step away from our routine to create, the views, the birds, the taste of the air are enough to jar us into new and innovative patterns of thinking.

For some, inspiration comes in a more tragic setting. Some of history's most compelling literature has been written in prisons or concentration camps. These dire conditions, like the grandeur of nature, push the mind into new arenas.

Some artists prefer to create in a commune, where a group of people come together to create in seclusion during the day and socialize and recharge their creative batteries by night. The New Harmony Project in Indiana is a place where writers can go for a few weeks a year and quietly work on their plays. In the evening, they meet and collaborate with directors and actors who read and perform the material written during the day. That kind of instant feedback can catapult the writer toward making quick and meaningful revisions.

Time Alone

The focused time alone to create is something that only you can create in your life and for yourself. It may sound selfish, but a life spent only on fetching and cleaning is a waste (unless, of course, you really love fetching and cleaning). Accept the fact that there will always be fetching and cleaning in your life and work hard to carve out a regular time when you can be alone to hear yourself think.

My trips to the hardware store are more than just an errand. They are a time of peaceful thought, when time can stand still and I can give as much attention to the directions on a bag of fertilizer as I normally would give to a movie script. It is time to be alone with yourself. A frightening thought for some, but for me this time alone to shuffle without pressures or cares through the bins of my hardware store is the stuff that feeds my creative spirit. With me it's hardware. With others it's books, theater, politics, or cooking. Whatever your area of interest, it really doesn't matter. What does matter is the care and feeding of your creative spirit in a very personal way.

After a century of industrialization and middle-American work ethic, it's very hard to convince yourself to step away from life for an hour or so each week and drift with the wind. Our logical brain protests. We should be working or at least balancing the checkbook or sorting laundry.

Once again in the pressure of daily life, we continually short-sheet our abstract brain. Don't do it. Carve out time once a week to do something that you want to do to recharge your creative batteries. Get away from your home or office into a new environment. Here are the rules:

1. You don't need to ask anybody's permission.
2. You must go it alone. Friends, spouses, lovers, kids are great but not now. After the obvious arrangements to care for your kids, spouse, or dependents (that's why they invented Top Ramen), leave them at home and go it alone in search of images and experiences that satisfy you. Only you.
3. Make your date with yourself a regular time so you are more likely to do it. We are schedule-oriented, so go ahead and schedule at least two hours each week (yes, a whole two hours) to spend with yourself. If you don't make it a scheduled date, you'll miss the opportunity.

4. Use this time to take flight into the previously unexplored. Do something different and challenging to
   your intellect. See an opera, eat eel, read Keats, learn
   to ski.

5. Make it a guilt-free zone: Aside from the normal eth-
   ical and moral boundaries that you might set for
   yourself, go ahead and don't feel guilty about it.
   Don't feel guilty that you spent an hour staring at one
   painting. Don't feel guilty that you bought a favorite
   lamp at a junk store or spent two hours playing computer games. No matter what your logical brain may
   scream at you, it's not a waste of time.

6. Make it a censor-free zone: Don't censor yourself. If
   you feel like joining an improv acting class, your logical brain will shower you with protest, but go ahead
   and follow your muse. Your creative spirit will thank
   you.

You may, no doubt, feel like an idiot sometimes, but you
are doing a truly important thing for yourself by creating
this crucial time alone for reflection and regeneration. So
embrace your inner idiot and do it. Allow yourself time to
really look at things, to really listen to a piece of music, to
really savor a fine wine.

And it doesn't always have to be fun or even happy.
Once I went back to the neighborhood where I grew up to
take a walk around and imagine what it was like back
when I was a kid. I could remember the pink Rambler
parked in our driveway and I could almost hear the sound
of my neighbor's mom laughing at *The Phil Silvers Show*
late at night. I remember the Little League baseball dia-
mond across the street from the parsonage where I grew
up. We bought snow cones from the neighborhood moms
who worked the snack shack on Saturday afternoons. The
PA announcer was a dad with a heavy Bavarian accent
and all the boys would giggle with delight when he said,

"He's rounding secund base unt heading for turd." That neighborhood walk was bittersweet, melancholy, and so evocative of a part of life that I'd forgotten.

Remember that this personal time-out is your time to collect impressions. Your personal creative expressions draw from your well of experiences and impressions. If your well has run dry then your ideas are soon to follow. Time out on your own lets you follow *your* muse and *your* interests and as such fills up your well of impressions so that you can again begin to express yourself in your work and art. Filling up your creative well is so important that it can't be left to chance. Your work depends on a regular and fresh flow of ideas into your brain and those ideas come from visceral real experiences. Your well needs fresh images, sounds, colors, smells—fresh thoughts expressed by writers, poets, filmmakers, comedians, politicians. All of these impressions give fuel to your creative fire.

Go to a coffee shop with a good book and camp out all night. Go to a newsstand and buy a paper from another city. I love small-town newspapers. I read a Sante Fe newspaper once where the lead story on the front page was titled: "Boy Detained for Laxative Prank." It doesn't get much better than that.

For a few dollars, you'll find that some activities are tried and true for recharging your batteries: art galleries, bookstores, travel, concerts, movies. It's just as effective though to recharge yourself without spending any money by visiting places like thrift stops, salvage yards, or even by watching people at the mall, or walking on the beach. Try not to shop, eat, or run errands. You do these things too often for them to be a replenishment for your creative soul. If you must do these things, then at least shop at a store you've never been to and eat an unusual meal. It's easy, just sample your mood and go. Go out by yourself once a week and play.

A lot of people stop and ask me, "Well Don, where exactly do *you* go to have some quality time alone?" So here, in response to numerous requests and letters, I have compiled a list of my favorite places to go for some creative fun.

Burbank on Halloween

Halloween is one of my favorite holidays. That's because we reveal our primitive side more on that day than any other. People who on October thirtieth may seem quiet and conservative, suddenly bedeck their houses in skeletons and headstones and walk around dressed like Elvis just twenty-four hours later. What a holiday.

I've always chosen something pretty safe for a Halloween costume. I don't look bad as a tourist (shorts, camera, black socks) or the lumberjack on the Brawny paper towel package (jeans, suspenders, flannel shirt, long underwear, stocking cap, roll of paper towels). At the animation studio, we'd always have these elaborate Halloween parties culminating in a costume contest. My Brawny paper towel guy never had a chance against the animators who would come in incredible costumes dressed as Malificent, Mount Rushmore, Mike Ovitz, or Gladys Knight and the Pips (although later I found out that the Mike Ovitz costume was really Mike Ovitz). Even though my costume always lost, I looked good in flannel and I came in handy for cleaning up spills.

Back at home the holiday took on the same feeling of wonder. We have a Halloween party every year in our neighborhood where children and their parents dress in elaborate costumes and come down to the main street to go trick or treating at all of the shops. We arrived late in the morning and went first to the kids' bounce house where Hulk Hogan and Frankenstein were bouncing around with Elmo and Buzz Lightyear. Next door was a hot dog stand where you could get free hot dogs from Napoleon and Big Foot and a soft drink from Superchicken. As we walked down the street to the center of the village, people were shopping in the stores and having their morning coffee. Wonder Woman was buying a donut for her little boy who was dressed like a hockey player with an ax in his head. A mom dressed like Elvira comforted her little Captain Courageous who had just been scared by the Yeti in the hot dog line.

Mr. Spock sipped on a decaf cappuccino while he read the morning paper. Across from him Superman and Spawn shared a cinnamon roll with Bob Dole (I'm not sure when Bob Dole became a revered Halloween character but I'm glad he did). These were normal people going about their day with festive abandon. It's as though people put a lid on themselves for three hundred sixty-four days and then once a year they decide to go completely nuts with self-expression.

There is a spirit that dominates Halloween that we lose the rest of the year. I'm not suggesting that boardrooms be overrun with executives dressed like the guys from *The Planet of the Apes* or that Congress be conducted in drag (although this would make a killer pay-per-view special). It seems that the collective creativity of the country swells up a little bit around Halloween time and that if we try, we could capture that feeling like lightning in a bottle and use it during the rest of the year. And what the hey, it might be fun to see a congressman trying to put a bill through the House while dressed in a Barney costume.

Oh the Doo Dah Day

A close rival to the creative spirit on Halloween happens every fall in Pasadena, California. Pasadena is a fairly sleepy suburb north of Los Angeles. It sprang up at the turn of the century when wealthy easterners came west in the wintertime to take in the warmth of the California sun, the air fresh with the scent of orange blossoms and the stunning scenery surrounding the Arroyo Secco.

The early turn-of-the-century settlers came up with a way to flaunt their newfound Eden to their families and friends back in the frigid East. Every New Year's Day, they covered their buggies and automobiles with fresh-cut flowers and paraded down Orange Grove Boulevard in a parade—the Tournament of Roses Parade.

Fast forward about eighty years. The current residents of Pasadena are now ex-easterners who moved here after seeing countless sunny Rose Parades on television while they were shoveling snow and scraping ice off their windshields. These neo-locals began tiring of the crowds and commercialism that the annual tournament brought to Pasadena, so they decided to spoof the Rose Parade with an irreverent pageant of the absurd called the Doo Dah Parade.

The parade usually starts with the local Harley-Davidson club astride their shining hogs. The riders wear pig noses. Then comes the queen of the parade: This year her majesty was a two-headed monarch named Queen Juliariana (lovingly portrayed by a mother-daughter team). The spectators run the gamut from families with kids and senior citizens on rollerblades to dogs with bandannas and buxom girls with cans of Sillystring. Occasionally the crowd at the Doo Dah Parade will show appreciation for their favorite marching units by showering them with a barrage of corn tortillas as is the tradition.

Following the two-headed queen (there's a phrase you don't get to use too often) is the first musical unit in the parade, Snotty Scotty and the Hankies. The band rides on the back of an old flatbed truck. Scotty sits on the hood belting rock-and-roll lyrics astride an eight-foot papier-mâché proboscis.

He's followed by a bagpipe band, the Bagel Street Hockey Team, and a precision marching group calling themselves The Bastard Sons of Lee Marvin.

The Doo Dah Parade is also a time to voice deeply felt political statements, and so among the marchers are a group called Legalize Ferrets carrying signs saying DON'T WASTE OUR TAX DOLLARS. To be honest, I wasn't aware that any of my tax dollars were going toward the oppression of ferrets or in fact that ferrets were illegal, but I was relieved to know that even ferrets have a voice in a democracy.

Another group called Pugs in Black march in protest of the harsh treatment of pug dogs in the movie *Men in Black*. Now to me, the sight of Tommy Lee Jones shaking a pug was one of the funniest things I had ever seen, but on this occasion it seemed only proper to sympathetically bow my head as if to say, "I feel your pain."

Some marching units are better than others. There's a

drag drill team, for example, made up of guys in evening gowns with makeup and false everything. Maybe I've seen one too many Milton Berle skits when I was a kid but this idea is getting old for me. Then there are a few belly dancers plying their trade along the parade route. This, too, seems like I've seen it before, and what's worse is that both the men-in-drag drill team and the belly dancers seem to evoke in the spectators an obligatory need to yell "Woooooooooooo!" (You know, that sound that the studio audience made when Al Bundy said something naughty on *Married . . . with Children*.)

These minor disappointments are eclipsed by the creative brilliance and raw energy of the next musical group, a personal favorite, the Red Elvises. Motto: "Kick-ass rock and roll from Siberia." My favorite drill team award went to the Barbecue and Hibachi Marching Grill Team. Each member of the grill team wears a personalized barbecue apron and carries his own grill or hibachi, complete with smoking briquettes and sizzling meat. Led by a drum major who twirls a lit tiki torch as a baton, the marchers wear Kingsford charcoal bags on their heads and beat an infectious cadence on their grills with their long-handled burger tongs and forks. An adoring crowd showers them with tortillas.

Hawaii

Who doesn't love Hawaii for a creative kick in the pants. Here's a place that's literally oozing with creativity and beauty. Lush jungles spring from incredibly fertile soil. Lava spews up from the center of the earth and hisses into the ocean to create virgin landscapes. The sea pounds the shore and sculpts the volcanic cliffs with ferocious tenacity. What a place.

And lest we forget, these are the guys that brought us things like luaus, surfing, the ukulele, and the pukka shell necklace. Not to mention the hula. I loved watching Ray Walston dancing in a grass skirt in the movie *South Pacific*. What a free spirit. Who knew you could have so much fun with a pair of coconut shells and a ukulele? The Polynesians, that's who. They knew how to live. White beaches, palm trees, fresh fish, and Jim Nabors *and* Don Ho. Now that's paradise. Sure, they've had their occasional cataclysmic volcano eruption or human sacrifice, but you can bet your poi they had a fine lifestyle, too. I used to think, This is paradise, *Bali Hai, From Here to Eternity*. If I could live anywhere during anytime, I'd live on Hawaii before the Europeans arrived . . . *with* modern medicine, of course.

But then I thought to myself, You idiot, everybody says something like "I'd love to live in ancient Greece . . . *with* modern medicine, of course." Well now, it wouldn't be ancient Greece if they had modern medicine, would it?

It's fun to do some imaginary time travel and think what it would be like to live in another era. This time travel may be a refreshing mental exercise, but at the end of the day, we are alive now, today, here, this minute. Place and time and creativity are inseparable. As much as I respect the art and culture of the islanders and as much as I'd like to live in Hawaii, I know I'd make a lousy Polynesian. I probably wouldn't last a day in ancient Hawaii. I'll have to be content with being a tourist and risk modern dangers like airport solicitors or death by taking on a terminal amount of sand in my swim trunks while trying to reenact that scene in *From Here to Eternity*. (And what's the deal with Burt Lancaster, anyway? He's kissing Deborah Kerr like there's no tomorrow, when suddenly an ice-cold wave slams into his crotch and he doesn't even flinch. Now that's acting.)

The Guy Store

Here's a place that doesn't exist, but if it did I'd rush there immediately for some male bonding. I like to go out shopping but I've noticed that there are lots of stores in our neighborhood mall that cater to what one might call ladies' things—not as in underwear, but things like needlepoint and potpourri. One store has lots of tole-painting supplies, embroidery floss, and paintings of warm candlelit cottages at dusk. The other carries doilies, teapots, coconuts, scrimshaw, and . . . no, wait . . . sorry, I'm getting them confused with Hawaii. Anyway, I do think it's nice that these "lady stores" exist, but I keep hoping that someday they'll open a chain of stores that sells everything that guys like.

Wouldn't it be a bonanza to open a Guy Store that sold nothing but cigars, combat fatigues, and deep-fried pork rinds? They could carry jumper cables, playing cards, Pop-Tarts, and Cheez Whiz and maybe for the sensitive man they could carry some books about wine, a copy of *Iron John* by Robert Bly, some Kenny G albums, and once again some Pop Tarts and Cheez Whiz.

The way I see it, they could even have seasonal guy stuff. For example, on the Fourth of July they could carry those hard-to-get firecrackers and M-80s. On Valentine's Day they could carry prewrapped lingerie with the gift card already attached and filled out: "To she who must be obeyed. Love you . . . Tigermuffin."

Along with the seasonal products you could have perennials like smoked meat, motor oil, fishing tackle, and eight-track tapes of Peaches and Herb. If you sold catapults, I don't think that men would ever want to shop anywhere else.

The Guy Store would also make the perfect place for your wife or girlfriend to shop for you since anything purchased there would be a treasured gift. And who knows, they might enjoy the helpful employees who give you a high five and a little slap on the butt every time you make a purchase. Choose from an array of video tapes about monster trucks, tractor pulls, bull riding, and one called *World's Coolest Things Dropped from High Places*. Nothing can compare to the grin on a man's face as he watches a bathtub full of tuna being dropped from the top of the Chrysler Building.

If women only knew how easy it is to attract a man and keep him happy. Just go to The Guy Store and get some bulk macaroni and cheese, nachos, beernuts, and a case of Pete's Wicked Ale and pop in a video like *World's Funniest Missile Launches Gone Bad*, then watch 'em come runnin'.

Europe

I think it's one of those rites of passage things—the first time you travel overseas. For me it was Europe with my friend Toad. I was so scared I stayed up all night the day before and threw up. I had been on a plane once before for a half-hour trip to San Diego. This was eleven hours across the world. Threw up on the plane, too. When I got there I had never been so tired. I checked into a Belgian hotel, the attic room was the size of my locker in high school. I remember the sounds were different, the cars were different, the food was different, the smells were different. It was like somebody played with all the adjustments on the TV set—it looked familiar but everything was a little bit off.

This was Europe, the land of the Beatles, Coco Chanel, and Toblerone. The centerpiece of western civilization. I felt so . . . well . . . American. You know, middle-class American kid in a foreign land making fun of the money and complaining about the food. The dialogue between Toad and me usually centered around body odor, food, and women with hair under their arms.

Europeans seemed to have a more mature sense of the creative spirit . . . architecture, art, music sprang up from the cobbled streets where Bach, Voltaire, and Goethe walked. Here it seemed like creativity was steeped in tradition. I felt very self-conscious, like all we do in America is think that the world revolves around TV, beer, football, and girls. Here in Europe amid the sophistication of centuries, the world seemed to revolve around opera, wine, football, and girls.

In Europe there was a sense of great pride and heritage. It is the birthplace of western music and literature, art and architecture. Each country seemed to contribute to the forward march of mankind. England fostered a great literary tradition, in Italy the streets were full of historic buildings and stunning art. Germany engineered great autobahns and the automobiles to navigate them. The French valued lifestyle above all. Their culture of art, music, wine, and cooking reflected that value. Toad summed it up one day while we were eating McDonald's hamburgers in Rome.

"In heaven," he said, "the police are English, the cooks

are French, the mechanics are German, the lovers Italian, and the politicians are Swiss. But in hell, the cooks are English, the mechanics are French, the police are German, the politicians are Italian, and the lovers are Swiss."

We had a good laugh knowing that we had broken the code and now understood all people.

Eight Seconds

My brother was about to turn forty. It seemed like the only right thing to do was to help him celebrate by getting away from home and going to one of the world's biggest sporting events; no, not the Super Bowl or the World Series, but the French equivalent: the Tour de France bike race. Ever since I was ten years old and raced my ten-speed around the streets of Bellflower, we had bike racing in our blood and now we would see it. An American, Greg LeMond, was in the lead halfway through the race, which was like a French football team leading the Dallas Cowboys in the Super Bowl at halftime.

We didn't have a lot of money so we stayed at the Hotel Jean Bart, a place that was described in the tourbook as "Parisian," meaning it had not been remodeled since the Allies liberated Paris. We arrived on the eve of the race's finale in Paris and after sleeping off our jet lag, we awoke and hustled downstairs for our "breakfast included." I asked about the pancakes: no. The oatmeal: no. The cinnamon rolls: no. It finally became apparent that the dinner rolls and coffee set down before us was the "breakfast included." The dinner rolls were well suited for street hockey and the coffee appeared to have been brewing since the French Revolution and had grown exponentially in strength with each passing year. Since we had no other choice, we chugged it cheerfully and headed out into the streets of Paris with a jolt of caffeine that made us move faster than Michael Flatley in one of those "Lord of the Dance" videos.

The July sun was already high in the sky and the temperature was warm, the atmosphere was festive as we headed out into the streets. People brought their families and camped out on the streets and sidewalks with elaborate picnics while waiting for the race to pass. The race route was lined with advertising banners and patrolled by gendarmes on motorcycles. We staked out a place on the Champs-Elysées, which was already about three-deep with eager Parisians.

This year the tour ended with a time trial. A time trial is a race against the clock. Bikers are released every minute or so and race as fast as they can on the course and the winner is the rider with the best time. Greg LeMond was fifty seconds behind a cycling legend, Lauren Fignon, a Frenchman. Before the racers arrived, the pre-race parade drove by to take advantage of the marketing opportunity of having a captive audience of one million bike-racing fans. Then after the giant inflated Michelin man passed out of view, the first racers started coming down the street at regular intervals. They had started one-by-one about thirty minutes earlier at the starting line near Versailles. Their heads were down, ears back, teeth gritted, and they were pedaling as fast as they could. The cyclists sped by every minute or so to the cheers of the fans, each followed by an entourage of sag wagons and team vehicles. Since the racers are released in reverse order, LeMond and Fignon were the last to hit the course. LeMond came first, we could hear the announcer herald his coming, but there was a murmur in the crowd. As LeMond came into view we could see why; he was tucked way over on his ten-speed with his arms pushed out ahead of him, holding handlebar extensions that kept his body in a low aerodynamic posture. On his head he wore a bullet-shaped helmet that seemed to split the air.

LeMond had to have every advantage the rules would allow, and no one thought of using aerodynamics to win a bike race. He whizzed by us like a missile. He was one with the bike. We heard the announcer in the distance. He was ahead by three seconds. Four seconds.

Then came Fignon. The last rider of the day wearing the yellow jersey of the race leader. The Parisian crowd erupted. But they also gasped at what they saw. His head was up and he looked tired as he fought against the wind, losing valuable time as he climbed to the top of the Champs-Elysées. LeMond had shaved fifty-eight seconds off of his overall time and was now, after two weeks and 2,500 miles of bike racing, in the lead by only eight seconds.

Fignon put on a heroic sprint down the boulevard to the finish line at the Place de Concorde and out of our view. The air was dead silent awaiting the announcement.

The word echoed over the loud speakers. Fignon hadn't been able to maintain his lead and LeMond won the race by eight seconds. We screamed. Game over. The eagle had landed. Good night, ladies, let's sing the alma mater and go home.

It was one of the most vivid memories of my life and the most vivid illustration of the race going not only to the most persistent but also the most inventive. We walked down toward the finish line to get a glimpse of LeMond as "The Star Spangled Banner" played over the public address system.

Creativity came to LeMond at the eleventh hour because he needed to ride the perfect race on the last day of the tour or he would lose. The next year, all the racers showed up to the time trials with handlebar extensions and bullet-shaped helmets.

Japan

Japan is a real eye-opener. Everything is as advanced and industrialized as in America, but created within a different cultural context. Simple things like sinks, plates, buses, signs, trains have been created from a different perspective. It made my head spin. Open your eyes to observe different perspectives.

I notice a lot of creativity coming from the Japanese lately. Japanese television, for example. They have the most outrageous game shows I have ever seen. Not shows like *Wheel of Fortune* or *Jeopardy!* They have these quasi-sadomasochistic truth or consequences shows. One time they made these three guys drink lots of beer and then stand on a block of melting ice looking at the ocean till they had to pee. And I thought *Tattletales* was good. The first contestant starts squinting and doubling over and suddenly he bolts to the outhouse and comes out happy as a clam. The other two contestants must have had bladders the size of Osaka because they stood and watched the waves come tinkling in for a long time before they had to excuse themselves.

What's the prize, you ask? That's the thing: Once the winner got a set of hot pads. One time they had guys lying on aluminum foil on the beach with magnifying lenses focused on their nipples and an ice-cold beer just out of reach. The winner was the one who could stand it the longest. And the prize? Dinner for two. Dinner for two and toasted nipples.

Yes, they are dominant in the field of sadistic game shows, computer circuitry, karaoke and sashimi, but I can't help but notice the fine new—how you say—toilets coming from the Empire of the Sun. I discovered this during a trip to Tokyo to promote the release of *The Hunchback of Notre Dame*. We held a press conference in a modern office building where I was about to stand up and speak in front of a group of fifty to seventy-five elite Japanese journalists and answer the usual questions like, "How many people does it take, how long does it take?" and the ever popular "Computers do most of this work now, don't they?" (The answers: six hundred people, four years, no.) We got to our presentation area early. I had a nervous stomach. It wasn't that I was going to follow President Bush's lead and barf on the dais. I just needed to freshen up a bit.

After rehearsal and before going on to answer questions, I retired to the men's room to powder my nose and there I saw it—the commode of the future. This welcome throne was all digital, with handy push-button selections with Japanese symbols next to each button. After some time I worked up enough courage and curiosity to start trying buttons even though I hadn't a clue what they did. First I found the button that should be called "power flush" (it lived up to its name) then to my delight the next button I pushed turned out to be "cleansing spray" (also living up to its name), followed by a refreshing breeze. What's more, it had a heated seat and best of all . . . a remote control! (Presumably in case you wanted to power flush while strolling some distance away.) Other features included a springtime rain and a lovely deodorant mist. It all amounted to the equivalent of a fancy car wash and detail job for a person's privates.

Here the Japanese have taken the most ordinary item known to mankind and converted it into . . . er . . . well . . . a piece of art. I returned to the stage with a spring in my step and a faint smile. The journalists all smiled back. They seemed to know where I had been.

3

THE

SPIRIT

If only God would give me some clear sign! Like making
a large deposit in my name at a Swiss bank.

—WOODY ALLEN

I'm a preacher's kid. I was raised in a parsonage that sat
in the expansive parking lot of Holy Redeemer Lutheran
Church. My father was a Lutheran pastor and my mom
played the organ and directed the choir. I lived in a world
of potluck dinners, prayers, and pulpits. God was a powerful thing to me then. After all, my God was the God of
Moses, Garrison Keillor, and ten million Norwegians.
Church was a happy place. When you called there, the
secretary would pick up the phone and merrily chirp

"Holy Redeemer" to a melody that was vaguely reminiscent of Woody the Woodpecker's laugh.

One Sunday morning I sat in my second-story Sunday school classroom with the smell of brewing coffee and donuts rising like demons from the kitchen below. My teacher Mrs. Holtzendorf casually read a Bible verse about creation that would change my life. It went something like: "In the image of God, made he man and woman." Wow. That *doesn't* stink. Suddenly, I'm some relation to God. A creative relationship. The same relationship that the potter has to his clay, the painter to his canvas, the baker to his bread. God made me like him!

It always seemed to me that God was crazy about creativity. Sure he must have had his frustrations and false starts—unicorns, dinosaurs, Jim Carrey—but just look at the successes: the painted desert, the northern lights, zebras, chick peas, Cindy Crawford, and the planet Saturn to name a few. And if God was crazy about creativity, and I was created in the image of God, then somewhere deep inside I must be crazy about creativity, too. And why not? Why couldn't the great creator enjoy creating?

Some experience God in nature. To others it is a force, a flow, a Tao, a higher power, a great creator, a unifying spirit. Some say God is an elderly man with a long white beard and huge bushy eyebrows, while others say that God is in every rock, tree, and creature. When I was really little I thought God's name was Hollow Ed since the Lord's Prayer clearly states: "Our father who art in heaven, Hollow Ed be thy name." I also remember hearing that he sits in Judge Mint, which presumably kept him smelling very fresh. But I was eventually set straight and at the very least I wasn't as confused as Toad, whose favorite hymn was "Gladly the Cross-eyed Bear." In the end, the only God I knew was the King of Kings who in the beginning created heaven and earth and now sat on his minty-fresh throne in the heavens.

Defining God

It seems so natural for us to have a direct and intimate relationship with God the creator, but as relationships go, this one has always seemed a bit strained. First, there was that Adam and Eve incident. As you recall, they got us off on the wrong foot when they couldn't help themselves from sampling the pippins in the Garden of Eden. Then there was that time when Moses went away to get the Ten Commandments and when he got back, everyone was worshipping this gold cow. Talk about embarrassing.

I could go on, but I think you can see, it's no wonder why God seems angry at us sometimes. And even when he doesn't seem angry, it seems impossible to get close to him. He seems so distant. First of all he's a monarch, a king, a lord. He's surrounded by his entourage of saints, apostles, and Della Reese with that Irish girl from *Touched by an Angel*. And secondly he's got to be unbelievably busy. Why would a God so powerful and secluded need anything from us except for our worship and praise?

God seems to be a hard thing for us to deal with. Most polls show that ninety-five percent of Americans say they believe in God. This is an astounding statistic since we can't even get ninety-five percent of Americans to agree on anything (except that the moon landings were staged by the CIA). But beneath this statistic there lies a hidden story. Even though we may believe in God, our belief is buffeted by uncertainties and confusion. How can this God be so powerful and secluded, and yet still be everywhere at the same time? (Bill Gates must struggle with this same dilemma, but then he has Windows 98 and God doesn't.)

We can't even bring ourselves to talk about God without using a string of powerful metaphors. God is called king, lord, judge, lawgiver, or at times he's a warrior, a lion, an eagle. Some metaphors speak of God with more tangible terms by calling him light, fire, wind, rock, and fortress. But so often our most dominant image of God is that of the powerful monarch—the creator who long, long ago built the universe and sits in judgment somewhere out there on his throne. God seems distant from us.

At the opposite end of the spectrum, there are also powerful and compelling metaphors that offer us an understanding of God as a near and present spirit. God the king may have presided over creation in some distant past, but God the spirit is here now, in every moment creating in front of our eyes in endless ways. God is frequently called a friend, a lover, a companion on our journey. Like a mother, God cares, loves, and nurtures us and even feels and participates in the suffering of the world.

The metaphors that we use to describe God the spirit (as opposed to God the monarch) seem very connected to our need for a partnership with a creative spirit. God becomes a cherished companion on our creative journey, where we see him more as a shepherd, a potter, a healer, a gardener, father, mother, and friend. Our knowledge of God is based, then, less on guilt, sin, and a distant glance and more on a living relationship that demands love, trust, fidelity, and intimacy.

God is already in a relationship with us and we need only be open to the companionship and comfort that this relationship can bring to our creative spirit.

You may argue that there are plenty of highly creative people who have absolutely no belief in God and of
course you'd be right. Some people feed off their strong
spiritual links not with God but with other artists, mentors, or peers. Others feed off of the spiritual connections
they glean from nature. Regardless of your personal beliefs, the creative process can only be enhanced if you
approach your art not as an isolated island but as an individual connected to the endless spiritual links around
you. If we are open, however cautiously, to the possibility of a spiritual influence in our creative life, then we
open ourselves to an unlimited supply of inspiration and
refreshment.

By seeking a direct link to God—creator to creator, artist to artist—what we really seek is a link to the creative
energy and flow that powers the universe. We were
formed from the stuff of the cosmos, we live and breathe
and eat the energy of the cosmos, why shouldn't we easily
and even instinctively draw on that energy to propel our
lives? It's the same energy that fuels the Milky Way galaxy,
the rise and fall of the tides, hurricanes, El Niño, the Spice
Girls, and Brian Boitano.

Now that we are pumped up with the power of the
cosmos, let's stop and consider our everyday up-at-dawn,
get-dressed-and-go-to-work life. We are creative all day
long. We create things like reports, coffee, stomach acid,
gossip, and we get a paycheck to thank us for our creativity. Not exactly communing with cosmic power.

We wish we could bring some creative power to our
office, or better yet, get out of the office and pursue our
dream. We probably feel like we are more creative than
we seem but can't quite tap into that creativity. Sometimes
we yearn to break into more overtly artistic pastimes like

writing or drawing. Sometimes we even look at people we feel are highly creative and long to have a life like theirs. A life full of openness and freedom.

Our days seem ruled by the chore-laden tasks of survival. We know that deep down inside we have good ideas but we don't know how to accomplish them. Sometimes we can't take a step forward even when we know specifically what we want to do. We sit and chant the modern-day mantra: If only we had the time, we could start painting or sewing, or playing the piano like we've always wanted.

Many of us had moments of great creativity when we were young but we can't seem to ignite those feelings anymore. Others have suppressed their own aspirations and invested themselves body and soul into the creative lives of another and are too afraid or weary to acknowledge their personal creative dreams.

In short, we will find any excuse possible to abandon our dreams.

Too busy.
The kids need me.
My husband (spouse, lover) needs me.
I'm too tired.
I'm too old to learn.
I'm too fat (thin, tall, short).
I'm too ethnic.
It's too selfish.
It's egotistical.
I don't have time.
I should be happy with what I have.

We are born with unlimited potential but if we aren't careful, we may never realize it. We put our precious physical energies into so many distracting things that we neglect to call upon them in the service of our own dreams and aspirations. We may even feel that the pursuit of a dream is a luxury item we can't afford. Even if we do raise our creative spirit from near death, we are hit with the realization that creativity does not always equal happiness.

Following your muse is fraught with upheaval. We suffer withdrawal from the predictable routine of our bland lives. We exchange a perfectly comfortable lifestyle for months spent trying to create at the typewriter, or at the canvas, or at the potter's wheel. You doubt yourself. You say, "People must think I'm a fool" and, worse, you say, "*I* think I'm a fool."

If you were searching for more creativity in your life three hundred years ago, I'd probably say, "Forget it, it's hopeless." You'd have been an indentured farmer who'd spend his whole life in the service of some fat guy with a powdered wig, so why bother. Heck, fifty years ago I'd probably have said, "Forget it, it's hopeless." You'd have been an indentured worker who'd spend his whole life in the service of some fat guy with a red nose and a cigar, so why bother. Things are different today. We live in an age of more tolerance, access, and openness than any other. Yes, there are intolerant, closed-minded individuals in every generation. There is always someone—some naysayer there to say "it can't be done." Take these examples from the past century:

Everything that can be invented has been invented.

—CHARLES H. DUELL, COMMISSIONER,
U.S. OFFICE OF PATENTS, 1899

Who the hell wants to hear actors talk.

—H. M. WARNER, FOUNDER OF WARNER BROTHERS, 1927

I think there is a world market for maybe five computers.

—THOMAS WATSON, CHAIRMAN IBM, 1943

The concept is interesting and well-formed, but in order
to earn better than a 'C', the idea must be feasible.

—A YALE UNIVERSITY MANAGEMENT PROFESSOR IN RESPONSE
TO STUDENT FRED SMITH'S PAPER PROPOSING RELIABLE OVER-
NIGHT DELIVERY SERVICE. SMITH WENT ON TO FOUND FEDEX.

If you look for them, you can discover naysayers and
obstacles everywhere. Though imperfect, these times are
the prime time for the spark of your creative spirit to shine
through. Besides, if we wait for circumstances to be perfect,
if we wait for our muse to speak, if we wait for someone
to help us, we will never begin. The circumstances will
never be perfect, your muse is a fickle companion, and no
one will help you until you make the first step.

So as much as you may be suspicious of these six lines,
I believe them to be true:

You're not too old.
You're not too poor.
Your spirit has endless energy.
You have a right to have an ego.

Your family won't think you're crazy.
Your dreams don't have to die with you.

Billions of souls have lived and died on this planet and most never had the choice to consider a more creative lifestyle as an option. Our twenty-first-century lifestyle affords us the option to have control of our schedules and control of our dreams. Our ancestors invested a lot of hope in us. Their dreams and yearnings, their genes and aspirations now sit within us like pent-up potential waiting to be released. The least we can do is take a leap of faith that those hopes were not wasted.

Joy

If there is anything bordering on a homework assignment in this book, this is it. Somewhere, somehow, find a group of young children at a preschool or kindergarten or around the house, and ask to observe them. Don't judge or label them, but observe them. Their emotions are right on the surface. Look at their joy and intensity. They bring enthusiasm to everything they do. Sure, they are full of insecurities and fears and occasionally even tears, but young children are little optimistic creation machines. They love to play. Playing makes them happy.

Once again we turn to Aristotle and the very core of human need: That thing that drives us onward to create is our pursuit of happiness. We might seek beauty, romance, health, money, and privilege but only because, after all is said and done, we expect those things to bring us happiness.

You can't plan joy. You can't put it on your calendar

and say, "A week from Friday let's go out and have some joy." Joy is not a place you arrive at. How many times have you caught yourself saying, "If I can just make it through this next week then I'll be happy." We don't arrive at happiness like some destination. In fact, the times that we focus on joy as a conscious target is when it becomes most illusive.

There is no road map that shows us how to be joyful, although bookstores and talk shows are full of people who seem to know. It's not an arrival that produces the sensation of joy but the total immersion in the journey of life that produces joy. Happiness comes from a very personal place inside that has to do with feeling deeply involved and in control of your life's journey.

Happiness doesn't always come with a ski vacation or a summer in Europe. The happiest and most exhilarating times in our lives don't often happen on a deserted Hawaiian beach . . . well, actually I take that back. Forget I said that last bit about the deserted Hawaiian beach.

Exhilaration comes from being stretched to your limits to accomplish something that was incredibly difficult for you. The personal feeling of accomplishment after the birth of a child, for example, or after the completion of an arduous project can create lifelong memories of happiness. Happiness can be born out of pain and struggle, out of striving for worthwhile things. When you feel that you are in control of your life and an active participant in the content of life, that's when you come closest to feeling a sense of joy.

Spirit on Fire

I would rather be ashes than dust!
I would rather that my spark should burn out in a
    brilliant blaze
than it should be stifled by dryrot.
I would rather be a superb meteor;
every atom of me in magnificent glow,
than a sleepy and permanent planet.
The proper function of man is to live, not to exist.
I shall not waste my days in trying to prolong them.
I shall use my time.

—JACK LONDON

Flip through the pages of your life and try to remember a time when you or someone you knew was literally a spirit on fire. I learned about passion from a trumpet player—a college music teacher who taught me about living a life with passion. Morrel Pfieffle (fortunately, parents have stopped naming their children Morrel) talked about jazz like one talks about sex. He spoke in hushed tones, with pregnant pauses, eyes sparkling and mouth turned up at the corner in an isn't-this-just-the-greatest smile. He would pick up his horn to play and the room would go silent. When Morrel played his trumpet, he would press it firmly to his lips and gently close his eyes as he manipulated the valves with arched fingers. The passion was palpable, the music was divine. I always felt like having a cigarette after his lectures. I learned a lot that year in college, not necessarily about jazz, and definitely not about sex, but all about passion.

In music school, the best musicians had one thing in

common. They practiced all the time. It wasn't talent, though they had it, it wasn't money or pedigree, it was the huge commitment to time alone with your ax (that's a musician's nickname for their instrument. I don't know why, but it's probably because it takes a lot of wood shedding to get any good at it).

I once took lessons from a musician who played vibes for George Shearing. I was amazed by his talent and ability to improvise. I would watch him again and again take long solos and never come back to the same idea twice. He'd move around and make up lines of melody and rhythm that would turn my impressionable head. Then it was time for my lesson. I was really looking forward to discovering the secret. I was going to learn how to improvise. First we did scales. Up the keyboard and down, then up a half step and do it again for a half an hour. Then he gave me my eye-opening homework. He tossed me a Charlie Parker album and said, "Go home and write down these improv solos and bring them back next week."

Written out? Copy? What? Where was my vision of dancing cleverly around the keyboard? I thought improvisation was the ultimate personal expression, why was I copying other people's solos? Weeks went on, I copied dozens of albums worth of solos and learned them all.

I smugly came to my next lesson ready to launch into a snappy version of "Bags Groove" in B-flat when he said, "Let's play it in D-flat instead." For all you non-musicians, that's the equivalent of saying let's repeat that last conversation we had word for word, but this time let's do it in Chinese.

After many frustrating months, I finally graduated to my own solos. My lessons taught me one important non-musical fact: Art comes after an incredible load of work and only one thing will see you through that work—passion.

Picasso, Degas, Frans Hals, and other painters spent a large part of their youth copying paintings and imitating the style of the great masters. Copying old master drawings and paintings can jump-start you and provide you with a strong foundation of reference. The same is true in architecture and dance and writing.

Degas said, "A painter must copy endlessly from the old masters and not until he has copied hundreds of paintings and studied the brushwork and color and composition of the master should he attempt to paint a radish from nature."

Sometimes we resist this help. Copying from the great masters of our craft makes us feel uninspired. What we are really doing is gaining insight into another person's creative journey. The more we can glean from the mistakes and successes of our idols, the more we can apply their journey to ours. We need to look deep into the creative lives of our heroes and see them not only at their best but also at their worst. How did Edison deal with adversity? How did Miles Davis sound on a bad day? What are some of Einstein's stupid ideas and let's see a bad drawing by Rembrandt. The journals and the accounts of how great artists struggled to express themselves can provide us with a valuable road map to start our journey.

For cryin' out loud, let someone help you. Enough of this stoic captain-of-your-destiny attitude. Don't try to find a creative place solely by yourself. Others have been there before you. Use their work as a beacon to illuminate your path. Mozart did it with Haydn, you can do it, too. Sometimes giving birth to your creative ideas is a long and painful process. You don't have to do it alone. Use a midwife to help. It's okay to seek out someone you admire and ask them for help and advice.

Mentors

A teacher affects eternity.

—HENRY ADAMS

There are many people in my life I consider mentors. Teachers who took a special interest in me or my older brother Jim, who taught me how to make a fine flatulent sound on my upper arm (which later got me in trouble in school: "We do not want to hear from your arm, Mr. Hahn.").

When I was twenty, I met an animator at the studio named Walt Stanchfield. Walt is the closest thing to a true mentor I've had. It's not that Walt drew better than everyone else, or taught better than everyone else (although he did both) but I admired him so much because he seemed to live better than everyone else. I liked the way he played tennis every day at age seventy. How he did paintings and sketches in the car without looking while driving down the freeway from his home north of Santa Barbara. I liked that he slept in the back of his van in the parking lot at work while he was in town and how he always seemed to have a bag of fruit with him. Walt was a character. He loved life. When he wasn't drawing he was playing guitar or making baskets in the style of the Chumash Indians. Walt's life was his art. He was forever intrigued with everything. When I first met him he was doing woodcuts (carving a drawing on a woodblock and printing it onto paper with ink). A year later he was mad about fauvism then later cubism, and later many other "isms."

Walt was interested in everything. When I was a budding artist at the studio, I took my drawings to him. I'd work for hours on a small stack of drawings that when flipped would form a simple animation action. I thought I was impressive. The minute I would take my drawings into Walt and he would put them on his desk, I would wince. What was I thinking. There was something magical about Walt's desk that made me see all my mistakes. Then again it could be his gentle manner as he sharpened his pencil and started talking: "Too many converging lines here, play this line straighter, watch this arc here, you're not thinking here." It was sweet and painful.

Years later, I asked Walt to come to London when we were studying to make *Who Framed Roger Rabbit*. The artists would crowd around him on the vacant third floor of an Edwardian factory building we rented. They would hang on every word and absorb every line of his drawings. When it came time to pose, Walt would become Jessica Rabbit. We had a leggy supermodel dressed up like Jessica, but Walt was the one who moved like her and helped us see what made her beautiful and sexy. On weekends, Walt and his wife would head out into the English countryside and come back on Mondays with a million stories about sheep, the price of Scottish woolens, and the silly-sounding places they had been, like Titsey, Shropshire, or Whaping Hedgehog.

Walt was a tireless sketcher. If he was away from his studio, he would render his drawings by dipping a brush into his cup of coffee at breakfast. He filled the pages of his sketchbooks with his "coffee" drawings. At home, waitresses who knew Walt would bring him two cups of coffee right away, one for drinking and one for painting. Tea worked as well when he traveled in England. Red wine worked at dinnertime. The drawings were loose and impressionistic and alive.

Walt collected things too. On the beach he would be facinated by interesting driftwood and rocks. Every Monday I would drop by his room and see his weekend collection. One week it was pinecones. The next it was photos of clouds, the next it was stories about some painting he saw in a gallery somewhere that stopped him in his tracks.

I had never been around someone like Walt. Part artist, part poet, part philosopher, part bag lady. But all passion, all seeing, all curious, all loving.

Get Charo on the Phone

Before I started working at the Walt Disney studio, I thought creativity and art were kind of a geek thing. Lots of my friends practiced the "commune" arts of pot throwing and guitar playing. Some did lovely needlepoint, macramé, or sand candles, and my Aunt Beverly once did an oil painting. But no one I knew, with the exception of a few teachers, seemed very serious about art. The artists I knew were hobbyists who pulled a shoe box from the closet on Saturday morning and toiled with their craft—almost apologetic about their art. Art wasn't important. Art was for amateurs—or so I thought. Then I met Woolie.

His full name was Wolfgang Reitherman. I had been at Disney for a couple of years and had known Woolie by reputation. He worked on *Pinocchio*, took a break to be a World War II fighter pilot, and came back to produce and direct *Jungle Book* and a string of movies in the sixties and seventies. One morning, I got a call from the front office asking me to go to see Woolie because he needed a new assistant director.

I sheepishly walked into his wing of offices on the second floor of the animation building, nodded to his secretary, Lorraine, and took a seat in his waiting area. That's when I heard him speak.

"Lorraine, get me Charo on the phone." Wow, so that's what a producer sounds like. He continued to talk. His side of the conversation was a sort of loud, monosyllabic artillery volley.

"Hey, how ya doin'!!... Ya... ya... ya... great... love to... yep... same here... you, too... okay... great... ya... okay... take care... you, too...'bye now."

After another brief phone call, I was ushered in. Part John Wayne, part Dean Martin, Woolie was a man's man. He always wore a Hawaiian shirt and held a big unlit cigar in his mouth which he chomped incessantly. He offered a big warm smile as he reached out to shake my hand. As he talked, his cigar got soggy so he'd reach into his drawer, produce a scissors, and snip off the end and start chomping again without missing a beat. Here I was pressing the flesh with one of Walt Disney's über-animators who looked like he could kick my butt if he wanted to. We chatted about our favorite movies. His was *The Guns of Navarone*, mine was *Chitty Chitty Bang Bang*. He was no hobbyist. Here was a man who was as comfortable drawing cartoons as he was flying a Spitfire or having lunch with James Coburn. He was no amateur.

Woolie's crew of animators was equally "grown-up." I was struck by the attitude these guys had about art. It was grown-up, unapologetic, matter-of-fact art. Everybody drew hard, laughed hard, worked hard. It was the first time that it dawned on me that art could be a grown-up thing to do. I wanted to be a producer. I wanted to get Charo on the phone.

Collaboration

In the fourth grade we got the chance to play a musical instrument for the first time. Our school district had hired two music teachers to go around to the elementary schools in the area and teach beginning instrumental music. Mr. Hobbs taught brass and Miss Bouvier taught strings. Miss Bouvier had a vague Russian accent and Toad and I had her figured for a spy during the cold war when she probably masqueraded as a string instrument instructor in order to torture information out of allied viola players.

Mr. Hobbs was American through and through. He ate peanut butter sandwiches, talked baseball, and drove a Chevy. We always had suspicions about the two of them being romantically linked—that they would meet after a long day of music lessons and make out madly with the 1812 Overture blaring on the stereo. But then again we had probably watched one too many Boris and Natasha episodes on *The Bullwinkle Show*.

This was an impressionable time when you learn a lot about your friends based solely on what musical instrument they chose to play.

Most of the pretty girls chose the flute (except for the really pretty girls who sang in choir). The girls who chose the clarinet were pretty, too, but usually wore glasses or had braces. The really geeky girls played the double reeds like oboe or bassoon and occasionally some poor girl would choose the trombone and elicit a flurry of suspicions that she was a lesbian.

The boys chose brass instruments or drums. In the first place, brass instruments had a thing called a spit valve. How cool is that!? It was a sure-fire chick magnet to be able to casually empty your spit valve and keep on playing without missing a note.

Who played what brass instrument was determined by lip size. It was one of the few things that I could think of in life that was determined by lip size. Small lips played French horn, big lips played tuba. Full lips, trombone. Normal lips, trumpet.

Drummers were usually shy and masked their timidness by carrying around drumsticks in their left rear pocket. This allowed them to play "Wipeout" upon request on the locker doors which was their only means to attract and impress the opposite sex.

Romance seemed to be determined by instrument, too. Flute players always dated trumpet players or drummers. Clarinet players would date trombone players (except for that girl trombone player who was always strangely alone) and saxophone players would date anyone who was upright and breathing.

Toad chose the trombone, not so much for his larger-than-average lip size but because it made a big and satisfying flatulent sound when you blew into the mouthpiece, which amused him to no end. I decided to play the cello.

The cello seemed civilized to me. First there was the tactile and somewhat primal satisfaction that came with drawing a horsehair bow across a catgut string suspended on a wooden box that was held between your legs. Secondly, no spit was involved. Lastly, as far as I could tell, lip size was not a factor.

There is no one in the universe more patient than an elementary school string teacher. The first virgin attempts to make a sound on a violin sound like an incontinent cat in heat. If you have ever tried to pick up and play a violin, you know what a miracle of the universe Itzhak Perlman is.

Our first forays into music were very important. We learned that if we worked together, we could communicate not with words but with our music. Most importantly it taught us lifelong lessons about collaboration. We learned how great it was to play together—that if we all followed the music, watched the conductor, and played our best we could all be proud in front of our families and even take a bow at the end of the evening.

Over the past twenty years, these lessons of collaboration that we had once learned in school are finally trickling into the business community and causing a revolution. It's a workplace revolution not based on the Internet, Dilbert, or the macarena, but on the transition from boss-centric offices to people-centric offices—a more level hierarchy of workers where outcomes are not dependent on just one human, but on the human spirit multiplied. Collaboration.

I did a television interview when we released *The Hunchback of Notre Dame* during which the reporter asked me this question: "Disney animation seems to have a lock on making successful movies. Other studios have tried and failed. Just what is the Disney secret?" The answer is the people—all the people. Like a large orchestra of individual players, when we come to work in the morning, we check our egos at the door like an overcoat that we won't be needing. Together the team becomes more powerful than any one individual could possibly be. The team is like a living, breathing, creative organism. The team knows all, shares all, sees all, achieves all, creates all.

This can be very hard to understand particularly when

trying to explain it to the press since the team does not photograph as well as Uma Thurman. Yes, there are producers, coaches, directors, quarterbacks, vice presidents, and CEOs. However, the revolution in creativity comes when those leaders support and challenge the creative team instead of dictating to the team.

Collaboration. It's the same in animation as it is in music, manufacturing, hotel management, or professional basketball: It takes a team to win the game. Not only the coach or the star players, but the entire team. Here are some rules for group creativity that might scare some people away at first, but they are worth careful consideration:

> Knowledge is everything and everybody needs the knowledge.
> Meet often, meet quickly.
> More meetings in the hallway, fewer in the conference room.
> Listen to everyone, no one has a stupid idea.
> No one person takes credit, all take credit.
> Reward the group, not the individual.
> Feed your idea, not your ego.
> The body must know its parts, learn about the other people.
> Less controlling hierarchy, more controlled anarchy.
> Never underestimate the power of free stuff (food, T-shirts, hats).

Collaboration doesn't make you a faceless contributor who labors for the good of the commune. It is crucial to remain a group of individuals that believe in and trust one another. This may sound impossible, utopian, superhuman, unworkable, but consider the alternative.

Tell them only what they need to know.
Please save all your issues for the weekly marketing
   meeting.
Stay at your desk.
Better to remain silent than to speak and appear stupid.
Reward the individual, shame the others.
Feed your ego.
Every man for himself.
Just do what the big guy tells you.

A Place to Socialize

Dave Spafford has been a friend of mine for a long time.
When I was twenty years old I moved out of my parents'
comfy house into a new apartment building a few miles
away. Dave moved into the same building. It was my first
apartment and I wanted to fill it with great personal expressions of who I was, so I set to decorating to express
myself. I had seen a picture in a magazine of classic bach-
elor crash pads of the era. All the heavyweights were rep-
resented: Burt Convy, Burt Reynolds, Burt Bacharach. I
wanted to be just like them, but sadly after my apartment
was finished, it was something closer to Bert and Ernie.
Well, it was home.

Dave, or Spaff as we called him, lived a few doors
down. We were constantly working. We had both just
landed jobs at the Disney studios the year before and were
now working sometimes ninety hours a week on *Pete's
Dragon*. We'd work until two in the morning shuttling
drawings, Hostess cupcakes, and beer up and down the
hallway of our apartment building. Next day we'd do it
all over again. Ten years later, Spaff and I ended up in
London, living in Camden Town and working with Dick

Williams on a movie about a rabbit who got framed for murder. Dave was the Daffy Duck guy. He animated the scene of Donald and Daffy Duck's piano duet in *The Ink and Paint Club*. Spaff became the social magnet of the studio. I learned two things from the British animators. They have a huge capacity for focused, hard work and they have a huge capacity for focused, hard beer drinking.

Friday nights were the best time to make the transition from work to beer drinking. The entire studio would escape to a pub and begin to sample the bitters and lager. I didn't get it at first. It was kind of smoky and loud. But this was the place where the real creativity took place. Here the artists could decompress from their long hours of seclusion at the drawing board and unload themselves. It was a healthy way to vent, complain, encourage, and counsel one another and eventually become a family.

The place to socialize and talk about politics and art was not a new idea. The New York intellectuals gathered at the Algonquin Hotel. The painters and writers of 1920s Paris gathered at La Cupole. The California impressionists had Laguna Beach, the rat pack had Las Vegas, and the beatniks frequented Ferlinghetti's City Lights bookstore in San Francisco. They all had a place to call their own and it was all essentially for the same reason. A place to unwind, a place to talk, a place to vent, a place to dream, and, yes, even bond together with friends.

I think Americans and particularly American men are all a little embarrassed to talk about bonding. Unless it involves football, smoking a cigar, or watching *Predator* on laser disc, we're hesitant to get together and talk.

After *Roger Rabbit* and the London experience, we all came back to Los Angeles happy for our ample parking and sunshine, but sad that we were missing the community of the pub. For years after our return, Spaff opened up his house on Friday nights so that the animators could come and hang out. Spaff's was an institution, a place to socialize, a transplanted pub in the backstreets of Burbank where body and spirit could be fed.

Community

Take hold of it and keep hold and let it pull you where it will.

—HENRY JAMES TO EDITH WHARTON ABOUT NEW YORK

When we choose where to live, we make a choice that affects who we are and what we create. The house we choose, the schools, shops, libraries, and restaurants we frequent all become the source of impressions in our life. All artists use their community as a palette for their work. The associations are endless: Cervantes's Spain, Jane Austen's Regency England, James Fenimore Cooper's American frontier, Dostoevsky's murky St. Petersburg, the isolated lives of the three Brontë sisters whose work is rooted in the wilds of west Yorkshire.

Some writers like Washington Irving were wanderers but would still bring their literary gift back to their beginnings. Irving was a product of the American Revolution, some say he was the first American writer at a time when professional writers were scarce in the new world. He would have long periods of expatriation where he traveled in England, Germany, France, and Spain, collecting folktales along the way. Two of his most popular stories, "Rip Van Winkle" and "The Legend of Sleepy Hollow," are actually Americanizations of German folktales reset in the timeless Hudson Valley.

Even when displaced from our homes, our work still is reflective of our roots. Robert Louis Stevenson spent the first twenty-nine years of his life in Edinburgh and then traveled to France, California, and eventually the Samoan Islands, but even in literary exile, his work was inspired by his Scottish roots. Victor Hugo, the symbol of French Romanticism, was in political exile in Guernsey when he wrote *Les Miserables*.

Sometimes writers are so strongly identified with a place that their names will become adjectives. For example, no writer has been more associated with a community than Charles Dickens and his haunting literary treatments of foggy rivers, debtor prisons, taverns, and coaching inn yards—all vivid recreations of the sights and sounds of his namesake Dickensian London.

Writers grow from community: Mark Twain's Mississippi, Ibsen's Norway, James Joyce's Dublin. Painters grow from community, too: Canaletto's Venice, Monet's Giverney, Van Gogh's Provence. Filmmakers grow from community: Woody Allen's New York, Barry Levinson's Baltimore, Ingmar Bergman's Sweden. You grow from community: Sally's Orlando, Jim's San Antonio, Toad's Bellflower.

When our creative spirit becomes stagnant or unfocused, sometimes we have to look back to the soil from whence we came. Where do *your* roots reach downward for nourishment? I looked around in the town where I lived to find the answers.

The shops along the little main street where I live aren't too fancy, but I'm convinced that you can find anything you need there. There is a pharmacy owned by a chatty elderly couple named Krapschutz. It hasn't changed much since the forties and sells the usual pills, salves, and ointments along with greeting cards, fountain pens, golf balls, and fifths of Scotch whiskey. They also sell notions. I'm not sure what notions are. I spent one summer working in a department store behind the notions counter and I'm still not sure what they are. I suspect they're those little essential items that you seldom think of but need every day like makeup pouches, swabs, Chap Stick, and *Yanni at the Acropolis* CDs.

Next to the pharmacy is a butcher and a produce store. It is so rare to find a butcher shop that's not a part of a supermarket that we're not sure anymore what to do there. There is a general notion that if you need a load of bulk meat quick, you go there. Or if you need something unusual like a cow tongue or a steak that is seven inches thick and isn't prepackaged in Styrofoam, you can get it there. Otherwise people just walk by and look into the window with slight confusion at the neatly lined rows of pork and beef, shake their heads, and move on to the produce store next door.

The produce store is also a product of another era. It sells only produce. Well, yes, there are a few canned goods, and a freezer full of milk but other than that it's a world of legumes, tubers, and squash. There are few other distinguishing stores in my village. There is a small Italian restaurant named Pizza Boy. It's the kind with red vinyl booths and wrought-iron light fixtures with the occasional bunch of plastic grapes hanging from black timber trellises. Pizza Boy is not like most contemporary Italian restaurants that serve risotto with arugula. It's more the kind of place where you can get a big plate of spaghetti with meatballs the size of your fist or a cheesy fettucine Alfredo that could stop your heart. I'm not sure why they call it Pizza Boy. Maybe they were trying to tap into the "boys" craze: Pep Boys, Bob's Big Boy, Poor Boys. Or maybe they thought that their original choice, Pizza Monkey, just didn't have the same ring.

Next to Pizza Boy is a video store owned by a sweet Korean couple. They have a few new titles hopelessly shuffled in no apparent order along with older well-worn cassettes. The only movies that seem to be meticulously grouped together in any alphabetical order are all the car movies: *Car Wash, Christine, Corvette Summer, Days of Thunder*, etc. This is presumably so you can run in and yell, "I need a car movie quick!"; otherwise it is a grab bag of titles. *Jerry Maguire* is next to *What's New, Pussycat?* next to *Cabin Boy, Shaft, Patton, Gandhi*, and *The Groove Tube*. I find the combination of titles refreshing. Sometimes I think the combined titles would make for better movies: *What's New, Cabin Boy?* or maybe a kid's Saturday-morning show: *The Shaft, Patton, and Gandhi Superhour.*

Across the street from the video store is one of the three car repair shops in our town. This one is run by Tony and his family. We have taken our car there for years and each time he replaces some part that I can't recognize, like the differential, rocker bars, or points. By now he's replaced so many parts that I'm starting to feel like it's no longer my car. In fact for a while I was suspicious that Tony was trying to steal my car, one piece at a time and replace it with one he didn't want. I smelled something fishy when we started out with a '95 Volvo and have slowly, piece by piece, ended up with something that looks strangely like a '77 Mercury Montego with a landau top.

Next to Tony's is a shoe repair store that sells handbags, too. On the same side of the street there are three beauty salons and one barber shop. Grooming must be important in our town since these places always seem full of ladies getting things done. The men go to the barber shop where Ben will cut your hair for six dollars and tell you all about the political conditions in the former Yugoslavia while you gaze at the Claudia Schiffer calendar or leaf through the latest copy of *Guns and Ammo* magazine. At six dollars, I find this one of the best values on the planet. Ben doesn't even own a blow-dryer or hair spray although he can give you something called a Vitalis head rub for an extra buck.

Oddly enough at the salons next door, only a small amount of the business that goes on inside involves cutting one's hair. They offer things like frosting, tipping, tiger striping, manicures, pedicures, facial treatments, and bikini waxes. They can wax your legs, armpits, face, and neck. One place even had an ad in the window for a full-body wax. I couldn't in my wildest dreams imagine someone waking up in the morning and downing a cup of coffee and shouting, "Bye, honey, I'm late for my full-body wax." But I'll keep an open mind. Luckily these things are handled behind closed doors in the salon where no one can see the act of full-body waxing and more importantly, where no one can hear the screams.

There is a coffee shop in our town and an antique store. I'm happy to say that there isn't a Starbucks or a Burger King on our main street. These chains are becoming so ubiquitous that parts of my town are starting to look an awful lot like parts of your town and everyone else's town, too. It's hard to feel like your community is a unique place.

I think it would be pretty easy to create a town these days if you wanted to. A hundred years ago, towns sprang up because there was a well or some sort of access to water. Maybe the location was a stage coach stop at one time, or a geographically unique setting. Maybe an itinerant preacher set up a church there. I wonder if today you could set up a town with a few well-placed phone calls. I bet you could.

I'd call Wal-Mart first since they can put up a store in the middle of nowhere faster than anyone. Then I'd call McDonald's and Burger King and maybe some exotic fast food place like Taco Bell or KFC. Then I'd call Boise Cascade to build some houses, Marriott to build a hotel for people who were waiting for their houses to be built. I'd call Texaco and Shell to build gas stations, Starbucks to supply coffee, Barnes and Noble for books, The Gap for clothes, and AMC to build a twenty-four-theater multiplex. For sinful pleasure I would call Häagen-Dazs and Cinnabon, and for entertainment Blockbuster Video and Virgin Megastore for music. Yes, with twenty calls, I could have my very own town. Eventually I could have some up-market stores like Macy's and even one day a Neiman Marcus or, dare I say it, my own shopping mall.

But somewhere along the line I'd miss something. I'd miss the personal qualities that I have in my town. I'd miss knowing that when I rent *Corvette Summer* from the Korean couple, my three dollars goes to them and not their home office in Duluth. I'd miss buying a seven-inch steak wrapped in butcher paper or getting my car tuned up while I'm having a full-body wax next door.

There are wonderful qualities to all of the businesses that operate as chains around the country. But every time a mom-and-pop business closes and a nationwide chain moves in it makes me a little sad.

It's hard for the corporate headquarters to know us by name or know what our needs are. Besides, Tony knows everything about my car and the Krapschutzes keep track of my preferences for nasal spray and whiskey. You are a product of your community and it is incumbent upon you to seek out and nurture what is precious and unique about the town in which you live.

The Audience

The audience is the observer, offering up their time and attention to experience your creation and inevitably offer up a conclusion about that experience. If you've decided to venture out of the safety of your creative womb and put your work in the critical spotlight of the audience, you should be prepared to deal with what they will tell you about your work.

The audience is trusting. The audience extends an unbelievable amount of goodwill toward an artist—at least at the start. Most people go into a movie theater with openness and a fair amount of trust and willingness to let the creator take them on a journey. That open accepting trust lasts only for a short time. From the time the first images appear and the sound track unspools, the audience is launched into a trance—that willful suspension of disbelief that allows us to believe in almost anything if presented convincingly. We know that dinosaurs are not real, but in *Jurassic Park*, we not only believe in them, we cheer when they eat that lawyer on the toilet. A good film completely steals your brain away from your own thoughts for a couple of hours.

The minute the audience starts saying to themselves, "That's stupid" or "Where did that plot come from?" they've become removed from the experience on the screen and start connecting with their own thoughts again. The most involving films I've seen have a way of keeping you so immersed that you don't question anything.

Take that same audience mentality into the art gallery. When I first started looking at paintings in galleries, I felt a need to have this big inner monologue with myself about the composition or the technique when all I really had to do was to simply open up and trust the creator. Just like films, some pieces completely swept me in and engaged me emotionally and others left me cold and swamped with thoughts about why the artist did this or that.

When we see an engaging piece of theater we are swept into the story by the emotional content of the piece. We don't notice the lights or the props or think about how much work the costumes must have taken. All those thoughts are last resorts that we might think only if our mind isn't in the story.

People love to be emotionally connected to art either through stories as in opera, film, or literature or through music or paintings that evoke an emotion. Even in works that have no narrative, like Brahms's German Requiem or a Beethoven symphony, we are nevertheless still transported to a place of incredible emotion.

And lastly, the audience is our spiritual partner—our link to humanity. When we write a poem or a song, or when we sketch or throw a piece of pottery, we are doing it to communicate life. This is never more apparent than in live theater. Theater is a tactile, real experience. It's not virtual or secondhand. We are there in the physical presence of dramatic gladiators. We feel the effect of their gestures, their sweat, their tears. We join together with the actors on stage and agree to reinvestigate the everyday with fresh eyes. At its best, we are transformed by the social experience of the theater and it becomes more than just a place of entertainment. It becomes a sacred place where humans share their humanity.

We choose to share our creation with the audience because it means something to us. We are beckoning them to sit down next to us and read or hear or see a truth we have found. We implore them to see through our eyes and feel our joy or sorrow, our hopes and fears. We invite total strangers to see into our spirit.

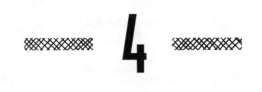

— 4 —

THE

FORCES

You're probably filled with the passion and desire to find a more creative place in your life. So now what? How do you master the forces that drive your creativity? Not forces like gravity, magnetism, or Richard Simmons, but odd-sounding forces like simplicity, splendor, and truth—now that's exciting. Here are a dozen creative forces that make my pulse race and my face flush with color. (I tried to focus on the greater forces of creativity. Of course there are other forces like dark chocolate, strong coffee, and Martha Stewart.)

Here's the list:

Craft
Light
Chaos
Balance
Curiosity
Composition
Simplicity
Spectacle
Surprise
Memory
Symbol
Truth

These forces are pretty universal to all creative endeavors. Great architects and composers, directors and scientists have worked with these forces either knowingly or intuitively to create their work and many a creative project was flawed because these forces were ignored.

Craft

Craft means ability, skill, knowledge, command, expertise, mastery. It can also mean slyness, cunning, cleverness, craftiness. Craft is knowledge cleverly applied. Pasteur wrote, "Chance favors the prepared mind." The more you know about your craft, the more force you can exert on your creations.

Everyone has to learn their craft. When life begins, most animals have some sort of innate and instinctive mechanism that allows them to survive and prosper. Horses know to give birth at nighttime to avoid predators. They carry some sort of genetic learning that their ancestors have passed on to them. Some animals have a special guidance system built into their genes. Geese know when to fly south, bats know how to navigate by sound, and some birds even know the patterns of the stars so they won't get lost during a nighttime migration. Humans have very few genetic migratory urges, with the possible exception of the male Thanksgiving migration from dining table to sofa to sleep off the tryptophan while watching some strapping youths pummel one another on a football field.

But unlike the average pregnant pony, much of what we need to prosper as human beings is not instinctive to us. We don't normally emerge from the womb singing show tunes and doing long division. We don't even know essential life skills like how to brush our teeth, or bunt a baseball, or that you should stop wearing black pantyhose after Easter. All of these things have to be learned.

To learn something we need to pay attention to it and attention is a very limited commodity. First, we need to carve out the time to focus on our craft and second, there is only a limited amount of information the brain can take in at one sitting.

We use tools or media in our quest to express our creative ideas and these tools represent a huge obstacle. Imagine you have an idea for a film. You can see it clearly in your mind. When you lie in bed at night you can hear the dialogue racing from the lips of a perfect willowy actress who walks down a tree-lined path lit in the glowing sunlight. It is perfection. Perfection in our mind, that is.

The first hurdle is to communicate the idea in your head to everyone so they can understand the film you see in your head. That pristine and perfect little impulse in your brain is about to begin a horrific and sobering journey. Your ideas must be put on paper in a script so others can read it and understand it. Next the studio hates the idea as written. As it turns out, they, too, have a pristine and perfect image in *their* heads and it doesn't match yours. You compromise and move to the next step where you must pick the actors who will tell your story. Gwyneth Paltrow is perfect to play the flaxen-haired maiden in your film but she is booked solid for the next forty years. You cast someone who looks sort of like the maiden in your head and then set off to find a perfect tree-lined path in the sunset. Instead you find the path lined with two trees, a cactus, and a billboard for Angelyne. Every step of the way, the perfect vision in your mind stumbles and hits the pavement. You are in good company since this is the age-old dilemma of creativity. The limitations of the physical world of lights and cameras and actors can never completely live up to the vision in your head.

Here is where craft becomes a force. We set out when we create to bring a mental image to life. The more we can master the brush and the paints, the more we can master the pencil, typewriter, saxophone—the tools of our trade—the more we can assert our creative vision. Almost immediately, as we begin to craft our creation, others begin to look on and comment. The balance now is between listening to the input from others and still staying true to yourself.

The mastery of your craft will allow you to flex your creative muscle with a certain confidence. The alternative to a strong craft is a personal expression that stumbles for lack of knowledge and dexterity with the media. The person without a foundation of craft can still create great things but the risk is very high that the abstract ideas in your head won't get communicated clearly and effectively. Craftless creativity relies on chance and novelty to communicate.

I met a man in New York named Lahrs Eriksen. Lahrs was an actor but he also liked clowning. I don't mean just clowning as in having a good time, but real circus clowning. Lahrs wanted to know everything there was to know about clowning so he read about it, and studied the great clowns of our time: Emmett Kelly, Red Skelton, Regis Philbin.

Lahrs went to the Ringling Clown School to study the craft. There he learned that clowns can specialize. They can be mimes, or perform a task like juggling or stilt walking. Or they can be comedians that write and perform comedic material.

At the Ringling Clown School they teach basic pie preparation and throwing as well as an introduction to the spit-take, and the art of dousing your burning butt in a pail of water while yelling the obligatory "My biscuits are burning!" or "Fire in the hole!"

Another class teaches rodeo clowning, or as it is now called, "How to Be a Diversion Artist." It takes great skill and knowledge to distract three thousand pounds of quivering bull wearing nothing but chaps and a smile.

If there are schools for clowning then surely there are places where you can go to learn everything about the fundamentals of your chosen craft. Finally, the definition of craft that is hard to teach is the sly, clever, cunning part. To be clever suggests to us a fresh unexpected way of doing things—an approach that skirts convention and exceeds our expectation. Learning our chosen craft is a lifelong proposition. You might even say it's a lifelong preoccupation. We can always get better and more insightful with our creative expression if we adopt the idea that we never truly arrive at a place where we can say with any confidence, "I know my craft." Artists attend a lifelong university, majoring in everything, minoring in nothing, and with one big commencement ceremony at the end.

Light

Light is everything. It is a life-sustaining force. It is a force at the center of nearly every religious and spiritual culture. It is the force at the center of science: Einstein's theory of the universe linked the four corners of Newtonian physics—space and time and energy and matter—to one thing. The speed of a beam of light.

It is a force in the arts. Society relies on innovators and artists to illuminate the truth. Creating brings things into the light. It illuminates and casts rays of light into the darkness.

In religion, in physics, in art, in life—light is everything. There is a prevailing and ageless concept of all humankind that light is a gift from a greater source. This belief spans nations and time and religious practices the world over.

Jewish scripture is full of references to light from God's first creational command: "Let there be light" to the Psalms "The lord is my light and my salvation; whom then shall I fear?"

Hinduism speaks of "enlightenment" as the highest of goals. Buddhism also speaks of enlightenment which transformed "endarkened" Siddhārtha Gautama into Buddha.

The New Testament of the Bible is full of references to light. Jesus of Nazareth called himself "the light of the world," and said, "He that follows me shall not walk in darkness but shall have the light of life." Islam's sacred text, the Koran, calls God the light of the heavens and the earth. Numerous Native American religions share a common thread of some sort of great spirit that is manifest in various colors of light. Others from ancient Rome to the Incas have worshipped the Sun God—light.

Light also represents heat and intense physical energy. The advertising world knows it as "don't sell the steak, sell the sizzle," the energy, the light. The orange light of the setting sun in commercials for cars, jewelry, hamburgers, and Kodak film solicit feelings of contentment, romance, and warmth at the end of the day.

Painters have long tried to capture light on canvas. Rembrandt and Caravaggio's powerful chiaroscuro made light advance from a sea of darkness. Film noir directors use the same conceit. Other artists like Turner and Van Gogh filled their canvases with abstract impressions of light and color.

And finally light can be a metaphor for purity and power. David Goetz, the art director of *The Hunchback of Notre Dame*, approached his work with a very specific goal in mind: to use light to capture medieval Paris. The source material for the film, Victor Hugo's novel *Notre Dame de Paris*, was a story of great contrasts. Light versus darkness, pretense versus honesty, silence versus cacophony, privilege versus poverty, hope versus despair. Goetz wanted to capture these contrasts of light and dark in the look of the film and so repeatedly, the background is divided into highly contrasting zones of cold, uncompromising darkness and warm, radiant light.

The absence of light is forceful, too. So much so that humankind has developed a way of dealing with the fears of the loss of light in the darkest days of wintertime: winter solstice. For thousands of years people have celebrated a wintertime festival at or around the shortest day of the year. Early pagan celebrations featured drunken demonstrations in the streets and the anything-goes festivals like the ancient French festival of fools where people dressed in costume and ran through the streets with drunken disregard (not unlike Super Bowl Sunday). These secular celebrations on the darkest winter days were eventually seconded by the Christians and their desire for a holiday to celebrate of the birth of Christ. The Christmas celebration with its yule logs blazing and evergreen trees with bright candles and ornaments became a reason to bring the light inside during the long, dark days of winter.

Our human rhythms are determined by the changing light of the seasons and by the light of the rising and setting sun. We respond in subtle and endless ways to changing forms of light. The manipulation of such a powerful primal force is central to painting, film, photography, theater, architecture, sculpture, and nearly every creative human endeavor from an explosive fireworks celebration to a candlelit dinner for two.

Chaos

Chaos a force? Yep, and a big one. The random nature of nature, of seeds blown into the wind, and lives changed in an instant is incredibly powerful. It's important to recognize the randomness and chaos of our thoughts and daydreams as a positive thing. The theories on the creation of the universe have their roots in a kind of divine chaos. Chaos is vibrant energy waiting to be harnessed.

It is not the chaos that creates, but rather how we choose to react to the chaos. In our accidental universe, the way in which we react determines our entire life path.

Chaos is the soil of creativity. It is the fertile ground from which all ideas and creation springs. The universe itself sprang from the chaos of a cataclysmic explosion and nature's creations come almost exclusively out of the chaos of the elements of earth, wind, fire, and water.

Our caveman brain associates chaos with disruption of order and an open threat to our comfort. We have done everything to protect ourselves from chaos. We have invented clocks, calendars, meetings, seasonal accessories, and day planners. We have standardized a once-chaotic language into dictionaries of uniform definition and pronunciation. We have labeled the universe with Latin names and created whole industries that teach management, order, and control. We can't imagine why we should have an interest in disorder, anarchy, and confusion.

Chaos is raw energy waiting for direction. If we try to direct the energy too soon, we can snuff it out. In our business or our personal or artistic lives, chaos is loud and scary. Our impulse is to shut it down as quickly as possible. But just for a brief and scary moment, let the chaos reign and try to listen to what it is saying. People never sit still during chaos. It is almost always an uncomfortable and unbearable thing for human beings to tolerate. People talk during times of chaos. They literally explode with ideas, opinions, and panicked cries for order. From that apparent panic comes a wellspring of deeply felt emotion and profound ideas for change. As uncomfortable as it is to bear these times, there is a galvanizing quality to a chaotic experience. The great ideas of politics, medicine, and art have often come from an unstable era when great men and women had been stirred into action by the chaos of their time.

In some cases, chaos comes slowly. Most projects start with a wave of careful planning, optimism, and hearty handshakes. The test comes when the project, along with the elements that were once carefully in place, all slowly erode into disarray. How we deal with that mid-project chaos separates the great from the feeble. We are not always able to put order into chaotic situations, but all we can hope for, as Willem de Kooning once said, is to put some order into ourselves. If we appreciate that chaos is the soil from which all creation springs, then we will learn to welcome it, if only for a moment, and listen to its cries. Therein lie opportunities of great risk, great stupidity, and great genius.

Balance

The definition of balance is simple—not falling over. Balance is seen in everything from the alignment of the planets to an ant carrying a leaf. Sometimes it's the balance between good and evil, or comedy and drama. And sometimes it's the balance between work and play or cheesecake and broccoli. Not surprisingly, much of art and drama come from an expression of imbalance in life.

You read a lot about stress reduction. Scientists are working on a "cure for stress." The problem really isn't stress; the problem is an imbalance of stress. The pain of stress can be a positive force in igniting our creative fire and can help drive us toward the completion of an idea. If you define stress as pressure, tension, and strain, then the opposite and balancing component would be release. The tension between characters in a play creates drama and the resolution of that tension usually means justice and a return to balance. Action movie plots are a convincing stream of tension and release moments.

The very act of creating requires an almost endless flow of tension-and-release experiences. Call it frustration and discovery, or research and breakthrough, or even impression and expression and you get the general idea. Stress is the tunnel through which we navigate to get to the other side.

Balance also has a million applications in business and the arts. In business it can mean a balance between product and marketing or investment and return.

Painters balance forms: soft versus hard, curved versus straight. They balance size, space, texture, and colors.

Composers balance their music with contrasting forms. Most symphonic forms of music balance a heroic opening with a slower second movement followed by fast movement and so on.

And then there is an issue of balance in life itself. The pages of art history are strewn with stories about imbalanced people and the art they create. This may lead us to believe that imbalance is a trademark of artistic greatness. It is not. There is no compelling evidence that you must be eccentric and nuts to be creative.

In color theory, artists talk about the color wheel in which all the known colors exist in a circle around one another. There are analogous colors that stand right next to each other (red-orange and yellow), complementary colors that oppose each other (red and green, yellow and purple), primary colors like red, yellow, and blue, and secondary colors that you get when you mix the primaries together (orange, purple, and green). Great paintings find a balance between colors. Even though the painting may be predominantly yellow or blue, it relies on all of the colors to make it complete. Corot used to put a small dot of red in the middle of a big green painting full of green trees and grass. This tiny red dot—a color that is completely the opposite on the color wheel to green—made his greens stand out even more.

Look for the opposite to balance your work. If you are an accountant, take up dancing. If you are a musician, follow the stock market. If you like to cook, go out and play a little football from time to time. That speck of contradiction will give your creations great range and color.

Let's say you're a businessperson and are trying to bring more creativity to your life. You should go read those books about ten ways to a better bottom line and such, but you'd do yourself a bigger favor by introducing a balancing element into your life. Pack up and travel to Tibet, read a good piece of fiction, get into a heated political discussion with your father-in-law, buy a foreign newspaper, eat a fine meal, paint a painting, or take a singing class. If we broaden our base of experience, those outside influences will begin to cross over into our day job.

From the time we attend grammar school to the time we enter the job market, society encourages the development of professional strengths and tends to discount mental balance and wholeness. We are even encouraged in unspoken ways to follow career stereotypes in education systems that freeze our attitudes about self into believing that art has no scientific basis or that business is not creative. Modern culture even rewards this thinking because it needs specialists to achieve its short-term goals. It's not natural to encourage balanced, unfocused education. This job orientation tends to limit our need to think expansively. From the minute we decide what our career will be, we focus in and disregard the brain's capacity and need for input from all of life's sources. We get frozen in our mental attitudes at a pretty young age. The task is to thaw out and reopen the interests that might bring more balance to your life and wholeness to your thinking.

Curiosity

> There was a child that went forth everyday and the first object that he looked upon that object he became. The song of the bird the water plants the flowers the pigs feet all became part of him.
>
> —WALT WHITMAN

When we were children, curiosity was boundless, or so it would seem. Everything was interesting to us: bugs, leaves, toes, trees, pigs, everything. As we mature, we are still furiously curious, but what we tend to do is to focus our curiosity into one field of work and then eventually down to one topic that is our life's work.

This kind of reductive focus—a progressive specialization of interest—is what makes the world an interesting place to live.

I have a friend. We'll call her Inge Voltberge. At a young age, Inge was interested in everything. She loved drawing and history and journalism and badminton. As Inge got older she became fascinated with government and over time decided to study law. After law school she decided to work for a major company as a lawyer in trademark infringement protection where she works today.

There is nothing at all wrong with Inge; in fact, she has followed the path of curiosity to a small corner of the legal profession that suits her well. She has gradually discarded the need to investigate other areas of life and has chosen

to follow her passion and an insatiable appetite for everything having to do with trademark litigation.

Now I enjoy a good trademark along with the next
guy. The Michelin man is nice and I like the Nike swoosh,
but I can't imagine spending my waking hours poring over
the latest in trademark law. Our ability to focus our energies into a specialized field of study allows us to take a
very expansive mental capacity and focus it on a tiny detail
of life with the hopes of contributing to society in a meaningful and welcomed way. The same happens to someone
pursuing the arts. It takes a great deal of focused concentration to master ballet dancing or oil painting. But the
greatest artists, be they a ballerina, a painter, or a trademark attorney, keep their focus small and their curiosity
wide. The nut to crack with creativity in any career is to
cultivate a lot of curiosity about a lot of things and then
bring the knowledge gained from that curiosity to your
very specialized chosen field of focus.

Composition

The composition of elements—active versus passive,
bright versus dark, loud versus soft, violent versus peaceful—is at the core of artistic expression, be it in a painting
or a master plan for a city.

I always think of cooking when I think of composition
(I always think of cooking anyway, but this gives me a
legitimate reason). Cooking ingredients are important. Stir
fry, for example, can be very artful. Before the creation
begins, the chef prepares a recipe and chops quantities of
onion, chicken, shrimp, squash, pepper, garlic, and spices.
Then the pan is heated and prepared with oil and then the

event happens. The chef instinctively mixes the ingredients in the right order and timing to produce a perfect dish where the chicken is done but the veggies are not limp. In a painting, the ingredients could be a tree, a cloud, a mountain, and a stream. The canvas and palette are prepared and the intellect is ready to assemble the ingredients. The painter instinctively mixes the objects in the right order and combinations to produce the perfect painting where the arrangement of objects and the application of the technique is just right.

A writer can work the same way. Before the writing begins, the writer prepares an outline and lists of characters, locations, research, and possible scenes in a story. Then the page is blank, the writer is poised, and this kit of parts is ready to be assembled, always searching for that perfect composition where the literary chicken is done and the veggies are not limp.

Simplicity

Simplicity. To some the word means elegance, grace, and sophisticated restraint. To others it means weakness, naiveté, and ignorance. In our culture, where our lives are complex and full of layers, we sometimes fear that simplicity—be it in design, or technology, or business planning—is somehow a sign of weakness. It is not.

To create with elegance and restraint is what every child does naturally. To him the sun is a yellow circle and a bird is a *V* in the sky. A house always has a chimney and a face has two circles for eyes and a triangle for a nose.

As we mature, there is a natural human tendency to add complexity. The details of life become very important and we often miss the simplicity of the underlying forms. As an adult, the sun is a confusing array of fiery gases that blinds our eyes, and the human face is so wondrously complex that we have given up trying to draw it.

In art school, much time is spent learning how to see the simple underlying forms. Great artists, and for that matter, great scientists and great businesspeople have the ability to look beyond the crushing details of the real world and see the simple underlying ideas upon which life is built. Can an idea be simplified down to one sentence? Can a drawing be made with one or two lines? Can a business plan be captured in one statement? Great things are built on simple foundations.

Great stories can be expressed in one high-concept line:

- A despondent man gets a chance to see what life would be like had he never been born—*It's a Wonderful Life.*
- A businessman risks everything to save Jews from the Holocaust by hiring them to work in his factories—*Schindler's List.*
- An outcast baby elephant becomes the star of the circus when he finds out he can fly—*Dumbo.*
- You killed my dad, you slept with my mom; let's fight—*Hamlet.*

There is great complexity and diversity in each of these stories. Being able to distill them down to a simple sentence provides focus and a united vision for the filmmakers and playwrights.

Business struggles with size and complexity all the time. A start-up company can become successful with a simple idea and a small group of employees. The capitalist system encourages growth. Then the challenge of maintaining success is complicated by more people, more meetings, more policies, more rules. The soil of creativity becomes so neatly tamped down that the once-spontaneous company that took pride in the fact that it started up in a garage and flew a pirate flag out front is now drowning in its own girth. The company lost track of the simple underlying idea that made it successful in the first place.

All this begs the question, "When do you stop?" When do you walk away from growth in business? Or is it okay to grow as long as you keep your eye on the core idea—the nucleus of your success? Simplicity isn't a course at the Royal Academy of Arts or the Harvard Business School. There is no formula for simplicity and the ability to recognize the simple expression of an idea. Knowing when to stop is as much a part of the creative process as nearly anything else.

Simplicity is elegant and even naive, but it is not a weakness. In a complex and detail-laden world, simplicity is a very powerful thing. Life is noisy and complex. Simplicity in a chaotic world becomes a strong and compelling counterforce.

A blank page in a cluttered magazine has power.

A silence in a symphony has power.

Vanilla ice cream has power.

Spectacle

We had a movie theater in Bellflower but I never really went that much. Movies were expensive and the combination of screaming kids and sticky floors kept my mom and dad away. The funny thing is, I never seemed to miss it until I had my first real movie theater experience.

One day, my sixth grade teacher, Mrs. Wills, sent home a notice to all parents that she was taking the kids to see a movie. But not just any movie. We were going to go see *Camelot* at the new Cinerama Dome in Hollywood. I'd never heard of that word before—Cinerama—but Mrs. Wills promised that it was something special, so we all signed up to go since Mrs. Wills certainly knew her special things. We had studied *King Arthur* for weeks before the field trip and knew all of the salient points of the legend and what to look for in the movie.

After a long trip in a hot yellow school bus, we arrived on Sunset Boulevard in the parking lot of this big domed structure. This was the time when Buckminster Fuller had made a big splash with his geodesic dome and it seemed like everyone was building one. The only difference here was that this one promised the biggest screen in the West.

Wow, I thought to my impressionable prepubescent self, flashing back to the jumbo dancing corn dogs at the Rosecrans Drive-in, this oughta be somethin'. We lined up in twos and filed in the front door where we were each given a giant-size popcorn and a bladder-challenging Coke.

As I walked in the door the first thing I noticed was that there was no screen. They were hiding it behind huge curtains. I sat next to my friend Toad and we happily jammed our mouths with popcorn and slurped generous portions of Coke while we waited.

On the hour, the lights dimmed and the curtains began to open. It grew quieter as the curtains parted farther. Oh my God, it's huge. The curtains were still parting and the white screen was becoming bigger than my backyard—bigger than the Rosecrans Drive-in. "Holy shit . . . it's massive," Toad whispered. "Oh . . . man . . . boy oh boy . . . this doesn't stink . . . oh, man . . . it's huge." I nodded in agreement, for who could possibly disagree with Toad's form of haiku?

As the opening scenes unspooled, we got our first glimpse of Richard Harris prancing about, smiling a wicked smile that easily measured ten yards across. He was ruggedly handsome with piercing eyes and a towering nose the size of Guam. Then came Vanessa Redgrave draped in flowing robes that seemed to fill my entire field of vision. She smiled a ten-yard smile, her beautiful eyes the size of sperm whales. The scale was meant to create a sense of spectacle and aura of respect for the story being told. My heart pounded in the jousting scenes as horses the size of Godzilla sprinted across the scene.

Mrs. Wills had told us about Lancelot but there was an audible gasp when Franco Nero appeared, resplendent in his fifty-foot-tall tights and sporting a codpiece the size of a Buick.

It was, to state the obvious, a spectacle. I drank up the movie pausing only to dash to the men's room and relieve myself from the enormous Coke.

I had never seen a screen so big, eyes so big, a Coke so big. There was nothing like this in Bellflower. Toad and I swore that when we were old enough, we would come back to Hollywood again together and see more spectacles one day. We never did.

Surprise

There is something in our genes that enjoys a good surprise. We love magicians, opening birthday presents, playing peekaboo with Daddy, hide-and-seek.

At the first hint of impending surprise, our pulse quickens and our eyes widen. The surprise could be wondrous or terrifying. A surprise represents a turning point in life. Something good or something bad usually happens as a result of a surprise.

A letter arrives in the mail and contains a check for ten thousand dollars. Another letter arrives in the mail and contains a notice that your husband is leaving you. Both are surprises and both are life changing.

We have had so many surprises in our life and the tension and release that comes with surprise is so satisfying to us that we look forward, albeit with mixed feelings, to the next one. As we grow older, it becomes more difficult to be surprised. The birthday clown just doesn't do it for us anymore. Our quest for surprise manifests itself in activities like travel, reading, or watching the evening news—all activities where we sit patiently waiting for the next jolt of delight or shock.

Magicians and filmmakers have always valued the basic human joy of surprises. Magic shows and horror movies are full of surprises. One thing that has united the great artists, scientists, dancers, and poets—indeed every great creative spirit—is the ability to surprise with his or her work. We come to a gallery or a theater or to a printed page with a certain expectation. Our enjoyment of the work is directly related to how the artist exceeds our expectation. The surprise can come in the form of shock or in the form of profound insight or in the form of comedic delight or physical human prowess, but the surprise is the thing.

Aristotle wouldn't have been surprised by this. It is our creative, imaginative side that helps us peer through the muck and mire of everyday life in search of the surprises that bring the possibilities for a happier life.

Memory

I'm in awe of people who have a great memory. I was out to dinner in New York with a group of directors and animator friends and we got one of those waitresses who didn't use an order pad, but simply took mental note of each person's order and then left without writing down a thing. It's not like we ordered a round of pizza and beer either. It was one of those restaurants with a menu full of choices and daily specials, so each person ordered an appetizer and a main course from a list of endless possibilities. How did she remember who ordered what? I figured she used one of those key word techniques you read about. You know, the thing where you use key words to remember someone's name. For example if you want to remember a name like Bonnie Brownlow you might associate Bonnie as the Scottish word for pretty or happy and Brownlow I might associate with something down low that is brown . . . like dirt. Bonnie Brownlow is now unforgettably Happy Dirt. Only, sadly, the next time I see her I can only remember the words *Happy Dirt* and stare blankly at her

for minutes thinking, Happy Dirt, Happy Dirt, Happy
Dirt. I can't for the life of me remember what it
stands for.

But I digress. Anyway, I'm convinced the waitress associated us with our order to remember who ordered
what: the guy with the black hair ordered seared tuna, the
guy that couldn't decide ordered the flounder, the short
guy ordered shrimp, the bald guy ordered the angel hair
pasta, and the guy who was middle-aged and forty pounds
overweight ordered the prime rib. I can't believe the memory this girl had.

She would even stop to answer questions people had
and she still remembered everything. I thought about hiring her for a while. She could follow me around so that
when I met people and forgot a name or something, she
could give it to me.

> ME: Oh, hello . . .
> MEMORY GIRL: . . . Bob
> ME: I haven't seen you in a while, not since . . .
> MEMORY GIRL: . . . we had lunch at the holidays.
> ME: How's . . . ?
> MEMORY GIRL: . . . your wife, Gail, and your two
> lovely daughters?
> ME: Are they still . . . ?
> MEMORY GIRL: . . . into ballet and soccer?
> ME: Maybe someday we can . . .
> MEMORY GIRL: . . . work on that joint venture with
> PBS and Britain's Channel Four chronicling the
> Olympic marathon runner from Swaziland.
> ME: See ya later . . .
> MEMORY GIRL: . . . Bob.
> ME: Oh, and . . .
> MEMORY GIRL: . . . thanks for the thoughtful
> message you enclosed in your birthday card. It really
> made my day.

Thankfully memory is more than names and details. We also have a very personal emotional memory. As a participant in life, we rack up a steady stream of emotional memories. We recognize a piece of music as being sad, the smell of a wood fire evokes home and hearth, a film reminds us of our own life and we can relate to it and be moved by it. Our brain tends to complete images, or phrases, or bits of drama based on our recognition of the situation.

Our participation in the art of cooking is profoundly physical since the results of creation are literally ingested into the body. One particularly American cooking ritual is the barbecue. We each have a favorite way of cooking outside, combining meat, briquettes, and oversize cooking utensils. Barbecuing became a defining pastime for American families. It was the barbecue sauce, however, that separated the men from the boys and in our house, we cooked exclusively with Mr. Cozart's sauce.

Mr. Cozart worked in the auto body shop of Spreen Cadillac, "Where the Freeways Meet in Downey." He also possessed the recipe for the most amazing barbecue sauce I have ever tasted. I had always imagined that he received it many years ago and that it was probably handed down to him directly from God Almighty in a brief ceremony held somewhere in the hill country of Texas. My brother and I used to try to guess what was in it. It was spicy and sweet, made with carefully protected ingredients that must have included mythic items like tomato sauce, brown sugar, steel shavings, and gun powder. I first tasted Mr. Cozart's sauce about thirty years ago. My mom managed to get the recipe from Mrs. Cozart one summer when the mister was out on a fishing trip and now we are in the possession of this peerless sauce from paradise. The thing that amazes me about this relatively simple culinary moment in history is that today almost thirty years after my virgin tasting experience, I can savor the memories and emotions of years of barbecues. I can see Mr. Cozart hovering over his briquettes, swathed in smoke, and wearing his GIVE THE COOK A BEER apron. Every time I taste Mr. Cozart's sauce, his creation lives on along with the flood of memories that surround it.

Time travel can be transmitted to all of our senses. We usually love the smell of fresh-baked bread or a newly mowed lawn because it transports us to another time and place and conjures up happy memories. We can listen to Gershwin and be transported to another time to feel the emotion of early twentieth-century life. We can read great literature and be transplanted to another time and place.

These sense memories are part of the palette of creativity. Artists, musicians, writers, and dancers all draw on these human sensory emotions to create pieces that are not just superficial exercises, but rather deeply felt emotional experiences.

My one and only experience as an actor was in my high school's production of Thornton Wilder's *Our Town* where I was cast in the less-than-starring role of the "belligerent man at back of auditorium." I got this role mainly because I didn't quite qualify for the two other bit parts, "woman in the balcony" or "lady in a box." My character was to stand in the back of the theater and shout a question to the stage manager (played by my idol, Harry Cason, a senior) and then storm back to his seat. I rehearsed my line in the mirror for what seemed like months: "Is there no one in town aware of social injustice or industrial inequality?"

It was opening night. The theater was filled with our pipe-smoking dads, and our grinning mothers who took this opportunity to wear their mink stoles and pearls. As curtain time came, our little brothers and sisters stopped running in the aisles and were shushed into their seats. The play began. Since my big moment came in the middle of the first act, I had what seemed like hours to review my line. Should I emphasize *social* injustice or social *injustice*? A throat clear might be nice. I wasn't sure what industrial inequality meant but if it was okay with Thornton Wilder, then it was okay with me.

My time came when after pages of beautifully delivered monologue, Harry Cason peered out from the stage and asked, "Are there any questions from the audience?" This was it—my cue. I stood up, cleared my throat, and paused a thoughtful pause. I felt the power of ten score people looking at me. The entire history of western drama seemed to rest on the padded shoulders of my borrowed Sears sport coat. I gathered my fifteen-year-old courage and shouted belligerently (I can take direction) from the back of the hall: "Is there no one in town aware of social injustice or injustial intemology?"

I sat down. Strangely no one seemed to notice my impassioned plea for something that sounded vaguely like unjust insect study. The play went on. But, ever since that day, I have had a deep-rooted admiration for actors.

There is an element of the actor's craft that is a force in all creative undertakings: sense memory. We have very specific feelings about our experiences gained through our senses. We have experienced our world with nothing more than sight, feel, smell, sound, and taste. That's it. When we approach the stage to create a performance or indeed, when we approach the piano to write a song or the stove to cook a meatloaf, we call upon sense memory to help us recreate our deep emotional feelings.

For years, I assumed that the dominant sense for me

and everyone else was sight. It seemed omnipresent, as though with sight alone the most important sensory information was available to me. But in time I learned that I really was a taste and sound man. My life's milestones could be measured more emotionally and specifically by the meals I ate and the music I heard. Music was such a direct way to my heart that relied not on sight but on the subtle vibrations of air that could move my soul.

Sense memories are powerful things. Jessica Lange said once that she carried a handkerchief with her onstage in *A Streetcar Named Desire* with the cologne of a childhood sweetheart, and whenever she launched into her role the smell of his cologne brought back feelings from her past that flooded her character. We can just mention a phrase that can elicit a strong sense memory.

The feel of freshly washed sheets.
The smell of ditto paper.
A candlelit dinner table.
Your mom's face.
Driving a new, clean car.
Out-of-control speed on skis.
Cat purrs.
A roller-coaster ride.
Crickets on a hot summer night.
An ice-cream headache.
Laughing children.
Fresh-baked rhubarb pie.
Cold, day-old pizza.
The shirt you bought in Hawaii.
The smell of Hai Karate aftershave.
Cold milk and chocolate chip cookies.
Strong coffee.
The taste of that sheetcake they bought for the office
    birthday party.

As a tool for the creator, memory, recognition, and sense memories are very powerful forces since they elicit a physical reaction to the creation. We bring our own emotional baggage to the art gallery, cinema, or theater. If we are truly engaged by what we see, we get not only to enjoy a show, but revisit the most profound emotional moments of our lives and bring them to bear on the work we are viewing.

Symbol

Here's an unexpected force, the symbol. A symbol is a thing that represents something. We use symbols to convey meanings too subtle or too complex for verbal language. In a way, every mark on a piece of paper can be and is a symbol. Something as simple as a pencil line can symbolize a horizon, a crease in a face, a cloud, a smile.

Art is symbolism. A painting my be symbolic of an idea or a political movement. Advertisers have long used symbols to communicate. A car is no longer just a car, it is a vehicle to attract the opposite sex. A fragrance induces imagery of the French Riviera with white drapes billowing in arched windows.

John Wayne in a cowboy hat, Marilyn Monroe with her skirt blown up, or James Dean in a T-shirt and leather jacket. Some actors have even reduced their name down to one gettable symbol: The Duke, Groucho, or more recently Cher, Prince, Madonna, Sting, Barbra, Oprah, Demi, Whoopi. All have brand-name recognition within a single word that symbolizes their character.

Motion picture marketing is in the business of creating symbols that make you want to go see a movie. The symbols can be romantic, comedic, action-based, or arty, but their sole purpose is to create an instant impression of the film and instill a desire to see it.

Symbols of family are extremely powerful. Myriad products have been sold using glowing, slow-motion imagery of kids and puppies playing on the front lawn. Small-town America is another powerful symbol. An idealized American life probably only exists in reality in very few places, but in our mind's eye, the notion of a small town with a steepled church and a bandstand on the green is linked to America as much as the symbols of Mom, apple pie, Uncle Sam, and the stars and stripes are.

One of the biggest treats of visiting Disneyland during my youth (aside from buying a giant dill pickle in the general store on Main Street) was the Circlevision Theater, then sponsored by Bell Telephone.

It was the kind of attraction that you didn't find at other amusement parks. Like Mr. Lincoln and the Hall of Presidents, it was meant to teach while it entertained, because here in the course of thirty minutes you could travel the great United States from sea to sea and get a glimpse of America like never before . . . in 360 degrees.

The queue area for the Circlevision Theater was a large room with benches where a perky phone company employee would talk about the virtues of long-distance calling. But the biggest attraction in the room was the booths around the edge of the room where you could try out new things like touch-tone dialing. The countdown clock which hung above the hostess reached 0:00 and the doors to the theater would swing out. We would usually be with someone who had never seen Circlevision before and I would educate them with considerable expertise that they should "hold onto the handrail because you might experience the sensation of motion even though there is nothing in the theater that moves."

Once inside, the automatic door would close behind us and some hidden computer would dim the lights and start the canned music as a sole spotlight appeared on some handsome college coed wearing a polyester midi with white go-go boots.

"Welcome to *America the Beautiful*" she would say to the hushed crowd who hung on every word of her well-rehearsed spiel. Then she concluded with, "Hold onto the handrail because you might experience the sensation of motion even though there is nothing in the theater that moves." I exchanged a knowing I-told-you-so look with my brother and the film started.

I saw *America the Beautiful* again just last year and for me it has become more than a brief travelogue at a theme park. It's like time travel. Not only did we hover over Niagara Falls and walk the front lawn of Mount Vernon, we also raced through the streets of Los Angeles on a hook-and-ladder truck and descended the perilous curves of San Francisco's Lombard Street to the groans of the audience. It was Los Angeles of the 1960s festooned with period cars and young men dressed up with butch haircuts and baggy pants, not unlike contemporary young men but with less body piercing. In San Francisco some of the pedestrian women on the streets wore gloves and dresses with petticoats. It is a film that still can transport me to another time when Florida tourism meant Cypress Gardens and Gatorland and Hawaiians farmed pineapples and did the hula. Along the way we visit Lincoln's log-cabin birthplace, an old seaport village in Maine, and Cape Canaveral in Florida.

The film builds to its final sequence in Washington,

D.C., where to the choral strains of "The Battle Hymn of the Republic," we focus on the imposing statue of the Lincoln Memorial and end on New York's Statue of Liberty with the combined voices of the Toontown and Mormon Tabernacle choirs belting the chorus of "America the Beautiful" to a full-blown let's-lick-the-Russkies crescendo.

As a kid, the symbols in that movie defined me and my country and I always exited the theater into the adjoining gift shop feeling a little more American than when I went in. The film was a shopping list of American icons: the Statue of Liberty, Mount Rushmore, the Lincoln Memorial. It was a living, breathing symbol for all things American.

Truth

The truth will set you free, but first it will make you miserable.

ON A BATHROOM WALL, LANGLEY, WASHINGTON

Truth is perhaps the most powerful and driving of creative forces. Creative people must have the desire to honestly communicate the truth about life as they understand it. Be it a painting, a photograph, a novel, or a play, artists can be society's primary keeper of the truth and a mirror of human values.

A lot of study has been put into the private lives of great artists. Most studies reveal that people who pursue the arts, apart from their drive to create, are really a pretty normal cross section of people in general. In some sense, it matters less what an artist does in his or her private life. What matters most is what he or she perceives. When we look at a painting or read a novel, we are looking for the unique perspective of the artist—a perspective that can not help but shine through and be reflected in the work. It is a reflection of what the artist sees as truth.

As creative observers, we are keenly interested in other people's art. We're eager to study and dissect it. We go to museums to try to understand art. What is art and how does one acquire an artistic hand? We are fascinated with the interpretation of the world that we receive from the artist. The irony is that art is an imitation, an illusion of life. It is a sleight-of-hand trick. Picasso says art is a lie that makes us realize the truth.

Most people would tell you that creative life is grounded in fantasy. Not completely. Creative life is also firmly grounded in reality. It is grounded in observation of what is real and truthful from the artist's perspective. Even the most abstract works of painters, sculptors, and dancers are reflections of the lives of the artist and their feelings on the given day they painted or sculpted or danced. We get frustrated at the abstract and nonsensical in art. We can't understand it. Well, don't try to under- stand art any more than you would try to understand a beautiful sunset or a cataclysmic storm. It's enough to en- joy the beauty or tragedy of life and take in its truth. The same holds true for creative expression. Trying to dissect and understand these creations won't help your appreci- ation of them any more than understanding planetary physics will help you enjoy the sunset.

It's true that we can always go back to a beautiful sun- set and study the atmospheric conditions that make it hap- pen, but we'll never forget the visceral pleasure we had when we sat there and watched the power of nature. We can study the ingredients of painting, music, cooking, or any human creation, but there is no harm in first openly experiencing the truth of the creation without a rush to comprehend its components. A creation represents one human being's unique perspective on life—one person's truth. It can be beautiful, naive, cynical, jaded, egotistical, modest, bold, tentative but it is unmistakably that person's truth. That is what makes art.

There is a phenomenon that artists talk about that I need to share with you. Next time you are in a gallery, pick a painting. Now stand in front of it in as near the place that the artist would have stood when he or she painted it. With impressionist painters, the pocket is an arm's length away, with some painters like Vermeer, it's very close to the canvas since he worked with very careful glazes, and with Jackson Pollock, the zone can be pretty far from the canvas since he usually stood over his work and squirted his paint from ketchup tubes. What you are doing by standing in this "artist zone" is feeling the energy of the painting converge back onto your eye. By standing where Degas stood, the painting fills your field of vision in the way it filled his.

I'm not superstitious and I don't have a New Age bone in my body, but when you stand in this pocket there is an unmistakable human energy that revisits us. It's as close as we can come to feeling the truth about the artist and the painting.

It's the same pocket that exists when you read a book and are on exactly the same wavelength as the author. You feel like the author is standing there whispering in your ear.

This bond between writer and reader or artist and audience is very personal. It's a very intimate relationship. Not all canvases or books will speak to you this way, but when they do it is pure truth—an intimate and direct link between you and the artist.

5

THE

FEARS

Life is short, art long, opportunity fleeting, experience treacherous, judgment difficult.

—HIPPOCRATES

Here I stand, equipped with an arsenal of forces. I am armed with hope, astride my best intentions, my eyes filled with passion, my stomach filled with acid—ready to be outstanding in my field, when suddenly I find my field is a battlefield. And there across the battlefield stand the long-faced naysayers ready to shoot me out of the saddle. These fierce warriors look right through me, their familiar names striking fear in my soul. Names worse than Attila the Hun, Bluebeard, or Dick Butkus. There stands Fear, and Insecurity, side by side with Withdrawal, Stagnation, and Mrs. Loots (my kindergarten teacher who said that if I ever wanted to amount to anything, I'd have to color inside the lines). Before I face this awesome phalanx, I take solace in the fact that others have faced these fears and emerged victorious.

The voice of Insecurity speaks to us with the measured surety of a mother saying, "I told you so" after we had tried to do something and failed. We start to think of reasons to avoid the risk of failing again. We have pointed little monologues within ourselves to validate our fears and we come up with reasons why we should never create again. Maybe some of these sound familiar to you.

> Everybody hates me.
> I can't draw (spell, read fast).
> I don't want to be alone.
> I only have a tiny amount of creative capital and I've spent it.
> I'll die poor and lonely surrounded by bad paintings.
> I'll drink, take drugs, and have sex.
> I'll feel terrible if I make money because I don't deserve success.
> I'll find out that I'm gay.
> I'll find out that I'm straight.
> I'll go nuts.
> I'll have to brood too much.
> I'll hurt my family's feelings.
> I'll never make money that way.
> I'll turn up some dark, sick side of myself that will embarrass me.
> I'll walk away from my family.
> I'm too old. If I haven't become a _____ by now, I never will.
> My family will leave me.
> My ideas are average or worse.

My parents will get mad.
My work will stink, but I won't know it and nobody will
    tell me.

We get so concerned about the public perception of us and
our art that we throw our hands up and say, "Why make
art at all if I'll have to hide my feelings?" Or sometimes
it's the opposite: "Why make art if I'll have to reveal my
innermost private feelings?"

For one reason or another, many of us began as highly
creative kids and have gradually become broken adult artists. As children we may start with warm support from
our mom and dad as we color on the kitchen table. As we
age, our creativity is put in check by well-meaning adults
who shower our fledgling creative efforts with unwanted
surveillance, unneeded evaluation, and contests where our
art, music, dancing, and writing are rated against those of
our peers. Society's need to reward the best shapes our
early years and we start to view our work as unworthy.

As a creative adult, we crave and need support, but it's
not always there for us. One of the animators at the studio
suggested we hire a mom to walk around from room to
room and compliment our drawings, give us hugs, and
feed us Rice Krispies Treats. We'd love to have our family
embrace our creative dreams, but it just doesn't seem to
happen that way. Either they don't get what we are trying
to do and think we're wasting our time or they are understanding and supportive and *we* feel full of guilt about
spending so much time away from them in the pursuit of
our art.

As artists and especially young artists, we long for
someone, anyone, to tell us we are worthy or on the right
track—to acknowledge our quest and share our failures.

Yet so often we don't feel support and we lose hope. We stop at the frustration part of the creative process and give up our dreams altogether.

It's easy for parents to envision their sons and daughters as doctors, firemen, teachers, and nurses. Much harder to encourage our daughters to be actors or sculptors or our sons to be painters or lion tamers. For most, the arts are only frosting on the cake.

In some schools, the arts are seen as nonessential and most often fall under the dubious title of electives along with auto shop and dance squad. The message is that the arts are a wonderful diversion, a hobby, but not real work. This message carries into adulthood and we find a job that requires us to put our creative dreams on a shelf—thinking perhaps we'll come back to them some day.

Fears and impossible obstacles all come down to one thing: Art is hard. If it was that way for Hippocrates twenty-five centuries ago, why wouldn't it be hard for you? Get over it. You can beat yourself up for years on end because you haven't acted on your dreams, or you can leap with conviction into your future and know that your parachute will open.

To overcome fear, we need to start with a more aggressive look at the life we've chosen for ourselves. Are you working in a chosen field that you love or are you marking time in a related field until you get your break? As a kid, did your parents and teachers encourage you to follow your muse or did they unwittingly fill you with doubts and low self-esteem? Are you truly happy with your chosen profession and just want to bring your creative spirit to the task or have you fallen into a comfortable job that pays the bills but leaves you spiritually bankrupt?

The creative journey is forward-facing. Even if you

have shelved your passion in the past, you can grab it and dust it off and take some baby steps toward a more creative life. Expect that you will be rusty and some of your first steps may cause you to stumble, but the pain and fear of those failures are a sure signal that you are moving forward once again. Write a bad screenplay, but write it now. Draw a few hundred bad drawings, but the sooner you get them out of the way, the sooner the good drawings will start to appear. Make a bad film, paint a lousy painting, write a hideous novel, but learn from it. And most importantly, there will be power in your decision to invest in your creative spirit and not push your talents to some subordinate place in your life.

Don't wait to get started. Lecturer Julia Cameron, author of *The Artists' Way*, responds to her students' concerns about the investment of time it will take to learn their craft. When they say, "But do you know how old I will be by the time I learn to really play the piano/act/paint/write a play?" she responds with a simple, "Yes . . . the same age you will be if you don't. So let's start."

Pressure

It was all set for three o'clock on a hot day in the fall of 1990. Angela Lansbury was scheduled to fly to New York to sing Mrs. Potts's charming ballad from *Beauty and the Beast*. She had worked tirelessly for weeks with a vocal coach on the subtleties of her performance. The day came, the orchestra was tuning up, and the control room was full of anxious songwriters and nervous executives. Three o'clock came and went and she didn't show up. I called her hotel—no one. Then word came.

Her flight's landing was delayed because of a bomb scare. I ran to the phone and checked with the airline. A phone-in bomb threat forced the plane to land en route and all the passengers had to deplane. The passengers boarded another plane and made it to JFK airport four hours late.

Angela had every reason to go to her hotel to rest and not show at all, but she knew the orchestra was there, she knew that the directors and songwriters were assembled, so after perhaps one of the most stressful experiences imaginable, she walked into the recording studio, greeted everyone cheerfully, and put her headset on and proceeded to sing. Three hours later, the result was *Beauty and the Beast*, the song that went on to win the Academy Award. I learned volumes from Angela's exquisite mix of work ethic and grace under pressure on that day in New York.

Pain

Pain. It's horrible and unbearable and, oddly, it's nature's blessing in disguise. Pain and the fear of it are nature's way of keeping us from stupid, self-destructive situations. Pain keeps us alive by acting as a warning system to help us locate and deal with physical and mental problems. But humans, more than the other animals, can recognize and overcome fear and pain with a conscious act of will.

We know that the process of creativity is full of disappointment, frustration, and pain. There is the pain of failure, of inaction, of humiliation. Nothing can really soften the pain of creation since each new project brings failures and humiliations of the heart. The creator has to find a way to live and deal with that pain—to even welcome it as a necessary adjunct to success.

We fear that during the creative process we will expose painful parts of our lives so when pain presents itself, we want to flee. Just as we might cover our ears for a loud siren or plug our nose for a bad smell, we protect our sensitive mind from possible pain by closing down. We stop short of expressing ourselves completely and honestly for fear of exposing some dark side or, even worse, some boring and stupid side. Innovative people learn to deny this self-protective instinct and stay mentally open to the impressions of life despite the threat of pain.

Sometimes we experience paralysis in the face of action. Feelings of stage fright or writer's block are less about the fear of failure and more likely to be grounded in a fear of taking any action at all. We may be searching for our big break in life, but when opportunity knocks, we sit tongue-tied. To overcome this paralysis, we need to embrace it and understand that all of these fears of expression are signs that you are opening up and arriving at a very vulnerable place where creation takes place.

There is pain, too, in the realization that what we have created is flawed. Finding the flaw in our work presents a choice. We can throw out all or part of our creation and start over or we can cover up the flaw and press on pretending it will be fine. Both are painful. Throwing out the product of your own hand seems somehow suicidal to the spirit, but even worse is the guilt associated with covering up a fatal flaw. It is the essence of creative life to find the flaws in our vision and flush them out in favor of a better idea. If we lose our critical eye and stop short of the self-criticism needed to create, then we are putting a throttle on the boldness and risk needed for great innovation.

The flaws in the work are part of the boldness required to create it. Flaws are the by-product of the process and when we recognize that the flaw is in the work and not in us—that the creator and the creation, though linked, are two separate entities—we can discard the flaw in the work without discarding a piece of ourselves.

The willingness to discard flawed work breeds a hope in the ability to rejuvenate yourself, and a trust in the flow of new ideas and optimism in the future of your creation.

Consider these words on the heroism of the creative journey by author Robert Grudin:

> Pain and fear of pain, finally, are the necessary conditions for courage. Creative achievement may seem solitary, even peripheral to society, but there is something genuinely heroic about it. And from an evolutionary perspective, it is they who most fully embody that form of heroism which gives force to the whole human project: the heroism of the seeking mind. It is perhaps this sense of heroism that makes creative endeavor so uniquely enjoyable, that justifies all the pain.
>
> —ROBERT GRUDIN, *THE GRACE OF GREAT THINGS*

Black Mondays, and Bad Days

It was the end of a very long October day and my office in an ornate Edwardian building in Camden Town was dark save for the warm light of my desk lamp (this is sounding like the beginning of a Miss Marple novel, isn't it?). I don't drink tea but that night it was late, and the English coffee machines made a brown, bean-flavored liquid that didn't quite qualify as coffee for me. So I stuck with the local custom and made a pot of tea as I pored over the production statistics on *Roger Rabbit*.

The numbers were bad. No one had made a movie like this ever before and the strain of the technique showed up in the form of really low productivity from the animators. The crew was the best that we could find in an age long before anyone dreamed of a *Lion King*. It was a United Nations of artists from Canada, Spain, France, Belgium, America, and of course the United Kingdom, gathered to work on this mysterious project about a rabbit who gets framed for murder. The average age in the studio was twenty-five.

Halfway through my Darjeeling, Peter Schneider called from Los Angeles. Peter had come from a successful career in the theater to be head of Disney animation at a time when the artists were making unfocused, lackluster films like *The Black Cauldron*. Since then, he has presided over a renaissance of the art of animation, but on that night he wasn't interested in anything but getting this movie done. He summoned me and producer Robert Watts to fly to New York. He would do the same with studio chief Jeffrey Katzenberg and the other filmmakers for a summit meeting (subtext: butt-kicking).

Twenty hours later, I was in a car watching the sun set on London evening traffic on my way to Heathrow with Robert Watts.

Robert was my idol. He had produced James Bond movies before he started working on films like *Return of the Jedi* and *Indiana Jones*. His producing philosophy, which he tossed off to me one day while munching on sausage rolls around the tea trolley, was this: Everyone here, from the producer to the lowliest runner, is here for one reason . . . to help the director tell a story. He had casually summed up the entire movie business with a few sausage-filled words and he was profoundly right.

To get to New York on time, the production booked tickets for Robert and me to fly on the supersonic Concorde from London to New York. The Concorde was for people in a hurry, people of power, and people of privilege. As I walked down the cabin aisle, the first thing I noticed, aside from how out of place I felt, was the lack of women and children onboard, and the second thing I noticed was that in the front row Princess Anne was sitting next to Itzhak Perlman. I was in good company.

As we took off, I looked out my tinier-than-usual window to see the dimly lit patchwork of the west country recede away from us at an alarming speed.

Everything about the plane was small and built for speed. The seats, the food, the flight attendants, everything was small and fast. Even the bathroom was small—so small that I had to arch my back and bend my knees limbo-style to fit in. It took me twenty minutes and seven of the ten basic yoga positions to relieve myself.

Once we had cleared Cornwall, the pilot floored it and I watched in amazement as the display at the head of the cabin indicated that we were traveling twice the speed of sound. Of course I asked myself a series of cocky questions based on my extensive knowledge of high school physics. Questions such as: "If I'm going twice the speed of sound then what happens if I talk? What if I turn toward the back of the plane and talk? If I make a phone call to someone on the ground will I have to speak very slowly for it to sound normal?"

I amused myself with these things until I noticed that the night sky was actually getting lighter. We must be catching up with the sun, I thought. Another round of

questions: "If we keep flying will we pick up an extra day
in our life? If we stay flying long enough will we actually
get younger?"

Mercifully we landed at JFK in New York. I flashed
Princess Anne a big Buccaneer smile and jumped into a
waiting car in time to see the sun set again, this time over
Manhattan.

The next day we would meet at the Disney offices in
midtown Manhattan. The studio had just acquired the offices from Pepsi-Cola and the boardroom was notorious as
the place where Joan Crawford held court during her brief
tenure on the board of Pepsi.

Robert and I arrived at the office by cab and dodged
ditch diggers and construction crews to make our way to
the front door. We huddled at one end of the massive
boardroom table and exchanged pleasantries with Bob
Zemeckis and Frank Marshall, who had flown in from
Los Angeles with Peter and Jeffrey. Tim Engel from finance, Marty Katz from the production office, and associate producer Steve Starkey sat with Ken Ralston from
ILM and I sidled up to Dick Williams as the animation
contingent.

The meeting began. The problem was this: We were all
working on a movie that we thought would be brilliant
and that we knew would be impossible to finish at the rate
we had been going. The creative and financial assets of
Disney and Steven Spielberg's company Amblin were tied
up in the results. And the results depended on animation.
What existed now on film was essentially an invisible man
movie that was waiting for the animation crew to add its
ink-and-paint cast of toons.

We talked about schedule and how to get it done and
we talked about the huge technical problems we were

having and then Jeffrey turned to me with a big grin on
his face and said, "Ya know what, Don Hahn will get this
movie done because if he doesn't . . . you see that guy
down there digging that ditch? If Don Hahn doesn't get
this movie done, that guy will be Don Hahn." He said it
with a big smile on his face—that same smile that those
banditos had in *The Treasure of Sierra Madre*. Then he said
something nice like, "And if he does get it done he can
have a job here for the rest of his life" or some such meaningless promise that you would never hold anyone to in
such a moment of rapturous prose.

It was the kind of moment you don't forget. I kept
hoping the dance squad would rush in and break the tension. The urge to projectile vomit was intense, but showing
restraint, I mumbled some sheepish pleasantries as everyone joked about my likely demise as a New York construction worker.

As the meeting broke up, we said our good-byes and
I dashed for the street with Robert Watts. After throwing
a "see ya soon" wave to the ditch digger in front of the
building, Robert and I went to a pier on the East River for
a helicopter ride to the airport and a flight back to London.
When the helicopter landed at the airport, we noticed people glued to televisions and stacked three-deep waiting for
telephones. It was October 17, 1987 . . . Black Monday—the
day the stock market crashed.

We did what all good producers do in the face of unsettling odds, we made jokes. We joked about the day, we
joked about the meeting, and to illustrate how pathetic our
condition was, we even joked about the stock market
crash. And as we settled into the seats on our Pan Am
flight back to London we agreed that tomorrow would be
another day. Robert reached over to pull the window

shade down and the entire window frame came off into his lap. It was the longest day of my life.

Impostor Syndrome

On days like that Monday in New York, you can feel what is referred to as impostor syndrome. It's that flash of insecurity that rushes over you like a chilling breeze and reminds you of your vulnerability. It reminds you that there have been times in your life when you turn on the creative tap and nothing comes out. You stop feeling like an artist and start feeling like you are an impostor posing as an artist but without any real pedigree or credentials.

Everyone has a brush with impostor syndrome from time to time. Here's one example: I met Arnold Schwarzenegger backstage at the Golden Globe Awards. *The Lion King* had just won the award for Best Picture and Arnold was the presenter. And while we waited for the press, I realized that I was standing next to Arnold. *Conan, The Terminator, Eraser*, this is a man whom I've seen driving a Harley through a plate-glass window while firing twin machine guns, piloting a harrier jet, kissing Jamie Lee Curtis, and muttering "I'll be back." Here I am, little Donny Hahn from Bellflower High School—the guy who smuggled a colander into bed in his pajamas—standing next to a man who is used to carrying a missile launcher in his pants. I spoke: "I just wanted to say I'm a big fan, I really love all of your movies." He smiled broadly and said in his charming Austrian drawl, "Oh, I loved *Duh Lion King*, too. You know it's so nice to have a film you can take your chooldren to, movies are so violent now a days!" He stopped a beat and slapped his bearlike hand to his forehead: "Vut am I saying, I go around shooting people for a living!" I was taken by the charm and humility of this former cyborg killer.

Great actors and directors, writers and scientists have all had a bout of impostor syndrome when they sit and wonder, "Who do you think you are? You don't know anything."

Our inner monologues can be pretty biting. We have a way of ripping ourselves apart with lengthy and accusatory speeches that confirm our worst fears—that we are worthless as creators. When we're done with ourselves, we turn on others. We call them lucky, talentless bozos, but what we are really saying to ourselves is, "Why can't I be like that? I'm an impostor, that's why."

When we try to right the situation by being more positive and harbor loving, caring thoughts about ourselves, we roll our eyes and interrupt with more inner "who-do-you-think-you-are?" dialogue.

What we need is a sense of hope and a sense of confidence in our creative lives. As sappy as it sounds, we do want to find a sense of self-love and trust that will allow us to move forward with our work. You might gag at the thought of having a positive internal conversation about yourself. After all, we've had years of internal talks about how lazy and unworthy we are, and it's become a very comfortable conversation to have. And every time we start saying things like, "I love myself and I deserve self-respect and a voice in society" we start sounding like Stuart Smalley on *Saturday Night Live* saying, "You're good enough, you're smart enough, and doggone it, people like you."

But somewhere deep inside in a quiet, personal, and

nonverbal place in our souls, we must believe that we've got something incredibly special and unique to offer. Our conscious mind may differ, our inner editor may object, our inner child may throw up, but beyond all of the voices to the contrary, you must believe in this fundamental truth: You are unique.

So here is a suite of positive affirmations that might sound cloying at first glance but to illustrate my point, try to pause for a moment and check your cynicism and then read these statements as though they were completely and irrefutably true.

> I am a creative being.
> God creates through me.
> By creating, I express the love and truth about life.
> I will not be afraid to express my creativity.
> I am worthwhile, my creative voice is important.

What if these statements were all true? I know it's much easier to believe that we are crass, cynical beings of questionable worth, but what if somewhere deep inside us we believed we had an important creative voice? What would we do then?

Would we write a novel if we knew people would read it? Would we paint fearlessly if we knew that our paintings expressed the love and truth about life? Would we work late into the night if we knew for sure that God was creating through us?

People will react to these statements in either a dismissive or a curious way. I hope you will at least be curious about the possibility that your unique creative voice is important.

Criticism

Attention to health is life's greatest hindrance.

—PLATO (427–347 B.C.)

Plato was a bore.

—FRIEDRICH NIETZSCHE (1844–1900)

Nietzsche was stupid and abnormal.

—LEO TOLSTOY (1828–1910)

I'm not going to get into the ring with Tolstoy.

—ERNEST HEMINGWAY (1899–1961)

Hemingway was a jerk.

—HAROLD ROBBINS (1916–1997)

Criticism is a powerful force in an innovator's life. If we internalize and believe every criticism, it can shut down our desire to create. In some cases, we will leap into a piece of work with enthusiasm only to suddenly lose interest near the completion of the project. This last-minute disinterest is our way of coping with the fear and vulnerability that criticism will bring by stopping the process altogether before the critics have a chance to speak.

We can't control criticism. It will come. It will come in the form of questions: "Are you sure that's what you want?" It will damn with faint praise: "Well, I certainly haven't seen anything like *that* before." It will try to make you change direction: "Ooh, I wouldn't have done it that way. Here, let me show you."

Kirk Wise, the codirector of *Beauty and the Beast*, talks about endurance in the face of criticism with a parable. The parable of the baker:

> There once was a baker who lived in a small and remote village where no one had ever seen a real cake before. He wanted to bake the most beautiful cake imaginable so that everyone in the village could enjoy it. He had an idea in his mind of just how the cake would look and taste when it was done, and just what ingredients he would need. And so he went to the grocer and bought some butter, eggs, milk, flour, and sugar. "You can't make a cake with this," the grocer said staring at his ingredients, "you can only make cookies with this." But the baker just smiled and went home where he began mixing his ingredients together. His neighbor the farmer came in and tasted the batter. "Is that what cake tastes like? I don't like it," he said, but the baker just kept on mixing.
>
> Then he put the batter into three round pans and put them in the oven. The village constable came by, peered into the oven and said, "Is that what cake looks like? It looks more like bread. Is cake like bread?" The baker kept baking and when the cake was finished, he stacked the three layers together on a plate. "That cake looks silly," his neighbor the seamstress said. "I've seen a picture of a cake and this looks nothing like it." But the baker kept going and frosted the cake with thick chocolate frosting. When the cake was done, the baker served up a big slice to all the villagers and they all smiled and said, "Oh, so that's cake."

The moral of the story is this: You may want people to see your work before it is finished, but they may misunderstand it and be critical of your half-baked cake. If we show our ideas too early, we might gain some useful input, but we also risk demoralizing comments that will be hard to overcome.

Understand that your art is revealing something very personal about you and that it's going to evoke a reaction (in fact, you should pray that your art evokes a reaction). Our instinct is to respond to criticism with a rousing defense full of articulate testimony designed to make the other guy look bad. But you don't have to respond. Most negative criticism is meant to be sifted through, learned from, and then discarded until next time.

As you cultivate the creative spirit in your life, there will always be other well-meaning people there to comment. They will want to evaluate you, reward you, control you, restrict you, and pressure you to conform to their way of thinking. But creativity is *your way of thinking*. You don't have to compete with anyone or please anyone unless you decide that you want to.

People will tell you anything to discourage you from creating.

> You'll go broke.
> You're not hungry enough.
> You'll go hungry.
> You're not tortured enough.
> You have no taste.
> Your work is meaningless.
> It's not as good as your last one.
> Only the paintings of dead people are worth anything.
> Writers are a dime a dozen.

It is important to point out that criticism is not truth but merely one person's opinion of the truth. Many a praised artist has dropped from the society pages into obscurity, and many a brilliant piece of music was panned at its first concert only to resurface as genius in the next generation.

Criticism is in fact a healthy component to the creative process. Here, then, is my foolproof method of dealing with the tough moment when someone walks up and criticizes your work.

1. Imagine that the critic is wearing no pants.
2. Listen to the criticism.
3. Don't feel like you have to respond.
4. Don't try to defend yourself.
5. Pluck out the valuable comments.
6. Discard the comments that you disagree with.
7. Thank the critic (they really are doing you a favor).
8. Consider what you'll do about the comments, if anything.
9. Weep openly in the privacy of your own bathroom.
10. Start back to work.

The combined voices of the critics in your head—both real and imaginary—make for a noisy accompaniment to creativity. At some point you must walk away from the cacophony and be left alone to joust with your soul.

> When you're in the studio painting, there are a lot of people in there with you. Your teachers, friends, painters from history, critics . . . and one by one, if you're really painting, they walk out. And if you're really painting, you walk out.

> —AUDREY FLACK, FROM A TALK WITH PHILIP GUSTON

Hiding in the Shadows

Sometimes our fear of criticism drives us to hide in the shadows of our friends and colleagues. We subordinate our own spirit and latch on to another person whose traits and creative spirit we admire. Our apologetic, creative spirit feels somehow validated in the shadow of these creative überhumans—you know, those people that we all know that love to be the center of attention, the eye of the storm. They are often charming, charismatic people who are highly creative and endlessly articulate, but for a creative person caught in the wake of their storm, they can be highly destructive.

They love a drama. They love to surround themselves with people who can support their needs, listen to their whims, observe their entrances and exits. And in the end, they will drive you nuts faster than an infomercial for the Psychic Connection Hotline.

We may have originally gone to seek this überperson's tutelage but then remained in the comfort of their shadow. At their best, these people might be famous, flamboyant artists who pride themselves on their larger-than-life style of living while feeding on the energies of their hapless followers in the most charming way imaginable. At their worst, they are people driven by power and fame who use and discard the people around them.

These people don't always seem harmful. In fact, they may seem like wonderful, driven, successful people who are worthy of following. But in following, we stall our own creative development. In following the überperson on his or her romp through life, we take up all of our energies serving their needs and with great exhaustion pronounce that we simply have no time for our own needs.

We find comfort in being close to such creative people and comfort in knowing that we ourselves don't have to risk or create. We might even feel uncomfortable at the thought that we might turn into this abrasive überperson someday—a thought that we loathe—and so we return to our subservient tasks, thankful for the opportunity to aid another person's greatness and relieved of the absolution of responsibility to express our own personal creativity. Next time you're tempted to stay in the shadow of someone else, call the Psychic Connection Hotline instead. It'll be a better use of your time.

Celebrity and Pedigree

Most creative people want recognition, and they think the lack of it smacks of failure. We put too much focus on fame. Fame is misleading. Yes, creative people do, on occasion, become famous for creating. It may be nice to be in *People* magazine or on *Hard Copy*, but it certainly has little to do with creativity. Many highly creative people are also highly creative in promoting themselves. The most noteworthy and quotable creative spirits of the last century were both great innovators and great at promoting and managing their images. That goes for Thomas Edison, Albert Einstein, the Rolling Stones, and Picasso. There is no discounting their accomplishments, but they also had the ability to bring their accomplishments to the world in a manner that the world craved and wanted.

There is nothing really wrong with self-promotion when you realize that it is related to the creative process.

The act of innovation is in itself an aggressive gesture toward society, challenging the comfort of the status quo. It is in effect saying, "You don't know what you're doing, here's a better idea." So in a way, the desire for self-promotion comes from the same impulse that drives us to create. Some innovative personalities are so self-assured about their accomplishments that they have the confidence not only to innovate, but to want to share those innovations with the world. Then it's up to society to accept the innovation or dismiss it until times change and the innovation becomes valid or useful.

Self-promotion without substance is usually quickly sniffed out by the public and I would like to think that great creative ideas also rise to the surface even in the absence of self-promotion and image management. We may discover a truth in our art that merits sharing it with the world, or we may discover something so precious that we want only to share it with our closest circle of family and friends. Some artists can't help but promote their work and others must keep theirs more private. You can't judge the worth of a piece of art by the fame or obscurity of its creator.

More important than any debate over the public or private consumption of a piece of art and far more important than the fame or obscurity of its creator is one thing: the art itself. Does it move us, does it challenge us, does it reflect the human condition back to us? This personal connection with the art eclipses the fame of the artist or the pedigree of the art.

We might be like the baker who loves to bake cookies and to sell them to everyone at the shopping mall, or we might be like the baker who loves to bake cookies and eat them alone in the kitchen while they're still soft and hot.

Both cookies taste good, both are worth making, both are highly coveted. Some are worth buying from stores and eating in public, and some are better enjoyed in one lone, rapturous moment, slumped over the kitchen sink with a steaming plate of soft chocolate chip cookies in one hand and an ice-cold glass of milk in the other.

I need to excuse myself for a moment. Pardon me, I'll be right back.

All right then, as I was saying: Please don't listen to all of the hyperbole that the fame seekers can generate. Hyperbole comes incredibly, extraordinarily, unimaginably easy to us in our age of media. In the last century we've heard things like:

> The French Army is still the best all-around fighting machine in Europe.
>
> —*TIME* MAGAZINE, JUNE 12, 1939

> Comet Kohoutek promises to be the celestial extravaganza of the century.
>
> —*NEWSWEEK*, NOVEMBER 5, 1973

> Rembrandt is not to be compared in the painting of character with our extraordinarily gifted artist, Mr. Rippingdale.
>
> —JOHN HUNT, NINETEENTH-CENTURY ART CRITIC

Nearly every movie ad in your local newspaper is bannered with bold, blazing adjectives from the critical press.

Even the most god-awful, horrid movies carry exuberant testimonials from critics: "THIS FILM IS EXTRAORDI- NARY," "BREATHTAKING," "AN INCREDIBLE CAST." All I can figure out is that the studios had to take these quotes completely out of context to make them work. What the critic really must have said is: "The fact that anyone in the unlobotomized world would even think of green- lighting THIS FILM IS EXTRAORDINARY," or "The snack bar had a BREATHTAKING assortment of Milk Duds and Junior Mints," or "The only reason I didn't run from the theater was that the guy next to me had AN INCREDIBLE CAST on his leg that blocked the aisle."

All of this hyperbole has a dulling effect on our senses. We want to know what critics think because sometimes it's critics who point out those in our culture who should be validated with the spotlight of fame and public recog- nition. At other times it's the groundswell of public sen- timent toward an artist that brings fame (as is the case of someone like Wayne Newton or Siegfried and Roy).

In any case, don't create just to be famous. I love what English cartoonist Gerald Scarfe says: "I don't want to be famous, I want to be fabulous." There are fifty thousand actors in Hollywood of which we know about a hundred by name. The kid on the street is more likely to know the names of the Teenage Mutant Ninja Turtles (Michelangelo, Donatello, Raphael, and Leonardo) than the names of the great Renaissance artists (Michelangelo, Donatello, Raphael, and Leonardo).

And besides, there is no compelling reason why people should care about your work. Most of what you will create is for your enrichment or is a stepping stone to other better, more insightful work. Maybe once or twice in a lifetime will you be recognized with the kudos of the public, so in the meantime, create for yourself. Create because you have to. Not to be famous, but because you are a living, breathing soul who must create or die a slow and boring death.

As a postscript, Frederic Remington was a tireless worker who painted numerous canvases for books, magazine articles, and galleries. He became one of the most famous and celebrated painters of his age. Yet Remington had a tendency to go over his paintings again and again. He would even redo large sections of paintings that had been finished for years but perhaps didn't rise to his expectations or didn't receive the kind of audience acclaim that he wanted. He even burned several canvases in frustration with his work.

Why should he burn his paintings and continually rework his old canvases, sometimes to a fault? Like all artists, from the epic muralist to the caricaturist at the county fair, Remington wanted what most artists want. He wanted to please. No quantity of fame or fortune could rid him of that wish.

Embarrassment

The first prerogative of an artist in any medium is to make a fool of himself.

—PAULINE KAEL

Take a moment and ask some simple questions to a group of people sitting around your home or office. Ask them about the marketing plan they're working on and watch them talk for minutes on end. Ask about their favorite football team or movie; more talk. Ask about their family; more talk. Ask them to sing their favorite song. Talk stops, pulse quickens, face turns flush. Now ask them to draw something. Pupils dilate, mouth dries up, internal organs fail. Then comes the nervous response, "Oh, no . . . I can't draw a straight line." (By the way, who can and who cares.) People get embarrassed when the spotlight is on them.

Ask a group of kindergartners to sing and draw and the air is filled with songs and crayons spring forth. What happened? Somewhere from the time we were five years old until now, we've slowly left the fun and playfulness of creativity behind. As adults, we have so separated ourselves from singing and drawing and dancing that we actually get embarrassed when we have to try. We'll sing in the privacy of our own car and with the help of a few beers, we'll dance at a wedding (especially if they start to do the chicken dance), but that's about it. A little voice inside stops us from expressing ourselves. We don't want to be humiliated.

Embarrassment can be incredibly painful. The pain can be debilitating and stop you from working. The pain can open wounds of insecurity and start a fresh inner dialogue of doubt:

> My work stinks.
> I'll be revealed as the impostor I am.
> I don't have enough time, so why start?
> I can't catch up.
> Criticism hurts, so why invite it?
> Just who do I think I am, anyway?
> Just shut up, nobody wants to hear you blab on about
>   your idea.

I'll look like an idiot.
It's a great idea, but I won't be able to present it well.
Nobody gives a damn about what I create, so why do it?
I'm blocked. I can't write (paint, draw, cook, dance) anymore.
I'm mediocre.

As a creator, you risk embarrassment and humiliation because your art requires that you step outside your comfort zone. All of the great innovators of history, and all of the great actors of history, and all of the great scientists of history have, at many times in their careers, faced embarrassment, humiliation, derision, controversy, and downright hate. You will, too. It will happen when you search for new ideas and fail. It will happen when you speak and are misunderstood, it will happen when the vision in your head can't be seen by the eyes of the others.

Junk

ZEPPO: The garbage man is here.
GROUCHO: Tell him we don't want any.

If you're like me, you get a lot of junk mail every day. Yes, occasionally there is a welcomed note from a long-lost friend or a surprise check from someone who owes me money, but most of the time, I get junk. I don't understand junk mail. The whole premise seems based on trying to trick you into thinking that there's something great inside the envelope.

Sometimes it's in the form of a window envelope that looks like there's a check inside. I opened one the other day. Through the address window you could see the words "Pay to the order of" printed in large letters above my name and address. There was a big federal looking eagle printed there too. When I opened it, it looked like a check for $35,000 but of course the words "non-negotiable coupon" were printed nearby in the same size typeface that they use to print the Lord's Prayer on the head of a pin. I must be on a mailing list labeled "incredibly stupid and gullible people."

Another junk mail envelope had used a typeface for their addressing computer that was supposed to look like the envelope was hand addressed. This way I would think it was a very personal letter from a dear friend and I would rush to open it first.

One junk envelope said "Certificate of Recognition enclosed—Please do not bend!" I must have fallen onto the mailing list for this demographic of "Ignored and unrewarded stupid and gullible people with low self-esteem." Another was a letter that looked like it was from the White House. The words "An invitation" were printed on the cover. It turned out to be from a political action group. I suppose they thought I'd rush to open it, thinking it was an invitation to sleep in the Lincoln bedroom. I'm probably on the demographic mailing list of "people who would respond to a bogus invitation to sleep in the White House."

What scares me a little is that these gimmicks must work, otherwise why would these organizations still use them? What do people do? Do they expect us to call up and say "boy oh boy . . . for a minute there I really thought this was a note from the White House! Oh brother, I sure didn't see a solicitation for money comin'. But hey, I feel so embarrassed that I think I'll send you some money after all, just because I admire your marketing moxie."

The topper was an envelope from a time-share con-
dominium that said, "You have already won one of these
three valuable prizes: a spectacular two-week Hawaiian
holiday, a fabulous new Chevrolet truck, a toaster." Now
you don't have to be a Rhodes scholar to figure that I've
won the toaster but I have to go to the sales office and
endure a four-hour interrogation before I can pick it up. I
wonder how many people gut out this sales presentation
just because they desperately need a new toaster. I've got
no experience with time-share marketing, but it seems like
a pretty flimsy business plan if you have to base it entirely
on people's overwhelming desire to have toast.

Junk can be alluring. It can look like found money, or
a note from a long-lost friend. It may try to trick us into
thinking something great is inside. It should be no surprise
to find that the same brain that produces masterworks can
also produce junk. At first glance, our creative ideas are
precious to us because, after all, we have created them. But
along with the breakthroughs we also tend to create heaping buckets full of junk.

The fear of junk paralyzes many people and stops them
from even starting their work. We get self-conscious about
our creations and think that our first brushstroke or our
first soufflé has to be perfection or that somehow we aren't
as talented or as gifted as the next guy. We are frozen in
our tracks for fear that at our very core we will create junk.

Well, it's true. If we just accept the fact that everyone
creates junk along with the good stuff—that the junk is the
natural by-product of the good stuff—then we won't be so
shocked and demoralized when we make something that
resembles horse stool.

We don't get much help from art galleries and museums here. Since most artists and old masters never release
their stinky work, it's normally the good stuff that makes

it to museums. Every once in a while, a museum will gather a show that exhibits the sketches, discards, and failed experiments of the masters and then you can see the human being at work inside of the mythic exterior.

I've always wanted artists to be brave enough to exhibit their junk along with their good stuff (myself not included, for fear of gross humiliation). Yes, show the beautifully painted final piece but also show the fifty sketches, the dozen stupid ideas, and the three failed attempts. That would create the real picture.

Learn to love the junk as a bridge to the better idea. Learn to understand its place in the process. It's okay to come up with a stupid idea. Nobody is going to frame it and stick it on the wall . . . well, actually that's not true. I once saw an exhibition of fast food that had been pressed between two sheets of Plexiglas at incredibly high pressure to create a sort of fast-food roadkill that was then framed and hung in a gallery. I thought that the squished Shakey's pizza and the dozen Dunkin' Donuts were boring junk but I found that the flattened KFC two-piece chicken meal with coleslaw and mashed potatoes was strangely compelling.

We need to be able to tell the difference between our gems and our junk. The creative process demands that we create freely, openly, and in large quantity. We shouldn't start a project by looking for only a few good ideas. Early in a project it's actually more important that we create lots of bulk ideas that reflect our feelings and thoughts. Then we can go back and winnow out the ideas to find the gold.

Junk, however, may not be junk forever and it should not get thrown away. Ideas that seem out of date and useless today might come into fashion tomorrow in the light of a new day. I also advocate a garage sale mentality: One man's junk is another man's treasure. The discarded ideas from the work of others can, when viewed in a new light, benefit and influence our work.

Take the case of a Dutch inventor named Cornelus Drebbel. Mr. Drebbel was actually a pretty well-known inventor back in the early 1600s although he never made much money at it. He invented a submarine complete with pressurized oxygen to breathe and had this hare-brained scheme to harness the sun's energy by focusing scores of mirrors on a central heating duct and then distributing the solar heat throughout London with an elaborate system of conduits. Pretty nutty, huh? It was, up until about thirty years ago when scientists started building massive solar collectors to harness the sun in much the same way Drebbel had envisioned it nearly three hundred years ago.

Cornelus Drebbel became one of history's forgotten men because, as brilliant as he was, society found no thirst for his ideas. And so as his wooden submarine sat rotting, and his solar collector drawings gathered dust, Drebbel finally met with success by opening a pub and serving up beer to his parched patrons.

Drebbel's story teaches four important life lessons:

- Creativity needs a receptive society or even the most brilliant of ideas will appear to be junk.
- Society has no way of keeping track of bad ideas or the work of "unsuccessful" innovators.
- Old junk can become new genius.
- When all else fails, serve beer.

Editing

I choose a block of marble and chop off whatever I don't
need.

—FRANÇOIS-AUGUSTE RODIN, SCULPTOR

Maybe it's stating the obvious, but humans are fundamen-
tally different from animals. Let me illustrate using man
and his best friend, the dog, as an example. My wife and
I once went to a restaurant by a lakeshore in a small mountain community where people enjoy bringing their dogs
with them everywhere. It was Oktoberfest time. The restaurant was a pretty little place that served German food
and beer on an outside deck surrounded by pine trees
overlooking the lake. We had ordered our bratwurst and
hot German potato salad and received our liters of Beck's
from an impressive-looking barmaid who could carry eight
beers at once and looked like she could bench-press a piano. About halfway through dinner, a couple came and sat
down next to us with their little fuzzy dog; I think it's
called a shih tzu, which is Chinese for "dog that pees on
the carpet when you get home."

At the first sight of my bratwurst, the dog bristled with
anticipation and began barking maniacally. His owners
were busy watching the barmaid bounce a drunken patron
when their dog broke loose of his leash, dashed under the
table, and thrust his fuzzy head up between my legs like
some sort of canine lap demon.

"Would you get your dog off of me," I said in measured tones sounding remarkably like Frank Gorshin's im-
personation of Kirk Douglas. His "mommy" turned and
smiled an oh-look-isn't-he-cute smile.

"It's your bratwurst," she said. "He just loves it."

"No foolin'," I shouted.

I pulled my thoughts together, smiled an I'm-going-to-kill-this-dog-unless-you-do-something smile, and uttered a controlled "please."

By this time my new lap buddy was drooling madly on my lederhosen. His owner came over and gave his pup a stern reprimand then turned to me and smiled, "He's just crazy about sausages."

I felt like saying, "Well, maybe next time you sit down you should yell, 'Watch out everybody! I've got a sausage-crazy shih tzu here!' " But instead we finished our meal, exchanged more smiles with the dog's owners, and left.

Dogs are so direct. They openly show their emotions to you no matter how they are feeling. It's no secret if the pooch is hungry, angry, horny, or sleepy; his emotions are there on the surface. We as humans, however, guard our feelings well. It would be unusual, for example, for someone to sit down next to you in a restaurant and upon viewing your bratwurst, leap to his feet and dash over to your table to begin drooling on your lederhosen. This rarely happens. We tend to do more self-editing than dogs.

A boy dog might see a pretty girl dog and sprint to chase her and bite her on the neck with frisky abandon. Humans occasionally do this, but are more likely to internalize their emotions and simply cast a stolen glance toward the object of their fascination.

We self-edit constantly, so much so that when it comes time to create art, we have trouble abandoning our "editor" and letting the more primitive hungry, angry, and yes, frisky artist show through.

It is the essence of creativity to find a place where you can let your hair down enough to feel your more primary emotions set in. If you are sad, to weep. If you are angry, to vent—not holding the emotions back, but letting them flow out on the surface in a stream of truth. This truth is from a deep place within you and is a precious human commodity that is unique only to you. Your emotions come from your life, your history, and your perspective and as such have enormous value.

Money

> When bankers get together for dinner, they discuss art. When artists get together for dinner, they discuss money.
>
> —OSCAR WILDE

When our brain thinks of money we think in terms of security, responsibility, solvency. When our brain thinks of art and innovation we think in terms of flying, dreaming, playing, and wearing silly trousers. It's no wonder that the need to pursue our art and the need to make money often fight in our little brains. Our left, doer brain tells us that work is a virtue and the harder and more dreary the job, the more virtuous we have become. It tells us that art and innovation are frivolous play and, although interesting, they don't pay the rent.

Our right, dreamer brain could care less. It longs to pursue painting, dancing, writing, and gourmet cooking. It soars when it's doing these things but it somehow gets frightened at the thought of having to provide security, too.

The dreamer in us has rarely been very sensible when it comes to money. Nevertheless, many of the great artists of the twentieth century have found a way for their work to be compatible with business. Companies pay millions to build the dreams of architects like Frank Gehry's Guggenheim Museum in Bilbao, Spain. Photographers like Richard Avedon, Ansel Adams, and Annie Leibovitz have found patrons in fashion or publishing. Celebrated painters from Michelangelo to Diego Rivera to Marc Chagall have painted murals under commission from large institutions. Even regional ballet corps and theaters mount endless productions of *The Nutcracker* and *A Christmas Carol* at the holidays because ticket sales can then support more fringe offerings during the rest of the season.

The flip side is that for every Avedon or Chagall, there are probably millions of photographers, painters, and other artists who have to live in the very tough economic realities of art. If Moses were alive today he'd probably have trouble getting published. Artists have always mourned the need for business as a companion to art. Even Beethoven hated it. He said: "There should be a single Art Exchange in the world, to which the artist would simply send his works and be given in return as much as he needs. As it is, one has to be half a merchant on top of everything else, and how badly one goes about it!"

The dreamer in us wants to believe that if we trust in our gift and believe in our passion that money will follow. The doer in us knows that money and creative vision are not always related. The financial reward comes when many factors are in alignment—factors like your personality, the art you intend to make, the compromises you are willing to make, the perceived goodness of your art, the receptiveness of the community, and of course, luck.

In the end, as with all creative pursuits, your attitude toward money and business is very personal. You will either trust your heart and leap into your work knowing that you won't sink if you are following your dream. Or you will carefully weigh your personality traits, tolerance for business, and willingness to compromise, and then move cautiously ahead with a careful plan. You will probably fall somewhere between the two, but don't let money be an obstacle to creating art.

What is money anyway, except beads that we exchange for the things we need? Sometimes I think we'd be happier if we just bartered. You know, exchange a service for a service. You scratch my back, I'll scratch yours. You paint my house, I'll do your taxes. I'll give you a loaf of bread if you wax my car. It works great unless you're a mime: You balance my books and I'll pretend I'm trapped in a small glass room. Money is here to stay so choose your personal style and either leap ahead aggressively or plan and take small cautious steps, but either way, don't stand still. Staying put is the one method that will assure your bankruptcy, both financial and spiritual.

Talent

The dictionary says talent is an innate capability—an aptitude, flair, inclination, or instinct for something. People talk about talent as though it were a measured commodity. "She's really got it," or "He was absent when they handed it out." The most sobering question that we dare ask ourselves is, "Do I have enough talent?"

Our thinking on talent is very prejudiced. We think talent in the arts is a God-given genetic thing, so much so that we don't teach the arts very much. We wouldn't dream of doing the same thing with reading, writing, or arithmetic. I've never heard anyone say, "Today's lesson is addition. I've put some pencils and paper on the table and you can go ahead and just use your imagination and think up some addition problems and solutions."

No, on the contrary, we prepare carefully and drill our children on math and language so that these skills are not left to chance. Why is it that we don't teach the arts in the same way? Well, you got me there.

There is a feeling post-Gestalt psychologists expressed that teaching art would damage creativity. Most all of the old master painters were carefully trained in the arts. In fact, the same skills needed in the arts—like perception and observation—are essential skills in other more academic pursuits like verbal and math skills.

The world is full of people who are endowed with stunning talents, yet they never produce a thing. Talent doesn't make the creation of art any easier, it doesn't absolve the artist from the work, or help weather the storms of change, deal with a frustrating medium, or help to insure artistic success. At best, talent gives a person a jump start—a firmer footing in the slippery soil of the arts. What happens after that is about the same for all artists. Making art is hard, so instead of sucking your lip away wishing you had more talent, try this: Take your passion, knowledge, and work ethic and throw yourself naked, with arms flailing, into something you love to do. Challenge yourself to know more, love more, feel more, and work more. Continue to learn, practice, explore, dream, and believe in yourself. Give your art your best effort and a funny thing will happen. Any question you had about your talent or lack of talent melts away as your personal creative self is revealed.

What Would It Matter?

When we were making *The Lion King* I met the Jouberts. The Jouberts are a husband and wife filmmaking team who camp outdoors for months on end in exotic-sounding places like Botswana to capture nature on film. In one of their most well-known documentaries, they filmed a cobra attacking and killing two baby lion cubs. I asked them the obvious city-boy question: Why didn't you intercede and save the cubs?

The balance of life is so crucial that saving the cubs might mean more lions the next year. More lions might mean more hunting and less game. The circle of life might go slightly out of balance in any number of unforeseen ways. The Jouberts' policy is to look, to film, but not to touch. One small action could affect generations of wildlife in unimaginable ways.

The moral of the story applies to humans, as well—one small action could affect generations of humans in unimaginable ways. Many give up on their creative hopes and dreams for a simple reason: What would it matter? You have no idea what it would matter and that's the point. There is no way that you can know the long-range effect of your creativity.

Physicists believe that nothing happens in isolation. All actions and inactions, no matter how small, interrelate. They call it the Butterfly Effect, based on the theory that if a butterfly were to fly into your room right now and get eaten by the shih tzu, the effect of that accident would be felt in other galaxies. The whole of the universe is interrelated in myriad and unimaginable ways.

Commitment

Writer's block doesn't just happen to writers. You may be tired or sick. You may be out of ideas or inspiration. You may just be stuck in the mud of life. The worst thing you can do if you feel stuck is to do nothing. When the well is dry, walk away, regroup with new research, inspiration, and a box of dark chocolate and try again.

Commitment is the key. Commit to returning and trying. Try writing more, try painting more. Diamonds are forged from intense heat and pressure and you have to look through a whole lot of slop and soot to find one, but when you do, you're rich. Ideas break through in the same way. If you were completely blocked and God dropped down from heaven and said, "Oh, you're not blocked, you just have to work through ten thousand boring, nonsensical words before you get to the next great idea," wouldn't you start writing? W. H. Murray talks about being blocked in this oft-quoted paragraph from his writings on the Scottish Himalayan expedition. Read carefully:

> Until one is committed, there is hesitancy, the chance to draw back, always ineffectiveness. Concerning all acts of initiative and creation there is one elementary truth, the ignorance of which kills countless ideas and splendid plans: That the moment one definitely commits oneself, then Providence moves, too. All sorts of things occur to help one that would never otherwise have occurred. A whole stream of events issues from the decision, raising in one's favor all manner of unforeseen incidents and meetings and material assistance, which no man could have dreamed would have come his way. I have learned a deep respect for one of Goethe's couplets:

Whatever you can do, or dream you can, begin it.
Boldness has genius, power, and magic in it.

Madness and Suffering

Creativity comes from a very primal place. As we grow
up, most people suppress these primitive voices, while at
the same time many highly creative people struggle for the
opposite—to stay in touch with their primitive selves. To
remain so in touch with these feelings sometimes means
that we walk a fine line between sanity and madness.

Plato wrote that creativity is "divine madness . . . a gift
from the gods." Van Gogh, Frida Kahlo, Jackson Pollock,
Edgar Allan Poe, Virginia Woolf—names that remind us
of greatness, madness, and suffering. Artists are driven to
create by their own psychological issues, and some have
bigger issues than others. Highly creative people may have
a greater sensitivity to emotional trauma than others. For
some, art becomes a salvation, a protest against death, a
way to struggle against adversity.

Anger, disillusionment and frustration can be vetted
and vented with artistic expression. Creativity is a con-
structive outlet and a healing force for painful feelings.
Learning how to paint, or play piano, or cook a gourmet
meal is more than just an idle use of your time. It is an
important cleansing force to help us deal with the problems of life and survival in a complex world.

Creating is a powerful way to face death and dying.
Even our own feelings of mortality take a mental backseat
while we are occupied with the act of creating.

Howard

In 1982, two fairly unknown song writers had written a musical based on an old science fiction film about a man-eating plant. One of the songwriters was a musician from New York whose father really wanted him to become a dentist, and the other was a lyricist from Baltimore. Alan Menken and Howard Ashman's work on *Little Shop of Horrors* won them international acclaim and landed them at Disney studios.

There, they collaborated on *The Little Mermaid*, which was seen as a triumph not only for the songwriters but for the Disney animation team, because along with 1988's *Roger Rabbit*, *The Little Mermaid* was the bellwether of a soon-to-be animation renaissance.

During the last few months of production on *Mermaid*, we asked Howard to collaborate with us on *Beauty and the Beast*. Howard was hesitant to work on *Beauty* for many of the same reasons we were. It had a second act that was all about a beast who came down to dinner every night and asked Belle if she wanted to marry him. She said no, he said all right, and he went away until the next night, when he came downstairs and started all over again. How do you make a musical out of that?

Over the next two years, Howard worked with us to do just that. He was sick and we didn't know it. When we got dispatched again and again to come to meetings with Howard near his home in upstate New York, I thought he was just being a diva. He was not. Howard had the HIV virus.

Eight of us, including directors Kirk Wise and Gary Trousdale, traveled across the country and checked into the beautiful Residence Inn in Fishkill, New York, to start working with the master—Howard. It was Christmas and we did the usual things a bunch of artists do in upstate New York. We ate dinner at Hudson's Fish and Ribs, then bought a gallon of ice cream and hot fudge and came back to the hotel to make angels in the snow and then watch *A Charlie Brown Christmas* while we made sundaes.

The next day we got together with Howard in an upstairs meeting room at the hotel—the kind of place where a salesman might discuss the financial benefits of siphon pump technology. But we were armed with sketch pads, storyboards, and coffee, waiting for the meeting to begin.

Howard Ashman was a tall and thin man who would show up wearing a white shirt and baggy trousers held up by suspenders like some character from *Inherit the Wind*. He walked in with a requisite bag of sugar donuts for us all and sat down. Howard, like many creative people, could have chosen to do many things in his life with great success. He happened to be a brilliant lyricist. But Howard could have easily been a trial attorney. He was extremely articulate and drew on an endless supply of examples from old movies, Broadway musicals, or his childhood in Baltimore.

Alan Menken was like a short-order cook. He served up dozens upon dozens of ideas, quickly abandoning the unworkable and expanding upon the good bits. Some songs emerged from well-trodden paths. Pastiche-sounding so they felt comfortable, almost as though you had heard them before, but always with an important twist.

The directors of *Beauty*, Kirk and Gary, had put together a rough scene for the opening of the movie. The ensuing discussion was like watching a doubles tennis match. Howard would serve up an idea. Gary would return, and all would volley until a high lob ended in a smashing win. It was all done with camaraderie and respect, but also with competitive passion. After weeks of writing, the first songs to emerge from Howard and Alan were the opening number "Belle" and "Be Our Guest." Howard was really nervous about these songs, so he traveled out to the studio to explain them while we listened.

Later came the ballad "Beauty and the Beast." We loved the song when it came in and some executives even wanted another verse, but Howard countered that he had used up every word that rhymed with *beast* except for the useless words: *yeast, feast,* and *creased.*

After all of the songs were written, Howard rolled over onto *Aladdin* to work on the song score. Even though *Aladdin* came out after *Beauty,* the *Aladdin* songs had been written years before and now Howard and Alan set to polishing their old score.

But it had become apparent by the time we reached recording sessions for the *Beauty and the Beast* ballad that Howard was becoming ill and losing strength. He had lost his voice and his phone conversations turned into strained whispers.

Howard had a singleness of mind that amazed me. By this time, everyone knew he was ill and he must have been in unimaginable emotional and physical pain, but he worked on. Even when he had lost his voice, he would sit in the back of the control booth and whisper his notes to Alan. Later we rigged up a system so that the music could be piped live to his living room in New York from our sessions in Los Angeles. He'd whisper over the phone while the whole room silently waited for his notes.

We added a last-minute song to *Beauty* called "Something There," a song that gave the objects' point of view on the romance of Belle and the Beast. Howard wrote a lyric that was full of whimsy and anticipation. Later that week he was hospitalized. I called him as often as I could and sent him dozens of innocuous things that I was sure he didn't care about—*Beauty* T-shirts, hats, and our prized crew sweatshirt.

I sent him regular videotapes of the film so he could watch the progress of the animation. He'd call me full of ideas and notes that were packed with vitality and authority.

I flew to New York in February of 1991 to show some reels of *Beauty* to the press. Kirk and Gary and I joined Roy Disney, Peter Schneider, and Jeffrey Katzenberg along with some of the animators to talk about the production. We rolled in a piano so Alan and Paige O'Hara could sing the ballad.

The reaction was something we didn't see coming. They didn't just love it. They adored it. They loved the story and the characters and above all they loved the music. That afternoon, Peter Schneider and I shared a car down to the hospital to tell Howard. We arrived at the same time as Jeffrey and David Geffen.

Howard was very sick and had lost his sight. When we walked into his room, it was the most bittersweet sight I have ever seen. Howard was lying there with his mom at his side, and he was wearing his *Beauty and the Beast* crew sweatshirt. We all stood and talked for a while and then shared the good news about the press conference. He was so happy.

One by one, Jeffrey and David and Peter said their good-byes and offered words of encouragement. Somehow I was the last one to go. Like the others, I bent over and whispered in Howard's ear. "It was great, Howard, you should have seen it, they really loved the movie . . . who'd have thought it?"

And then in true fashion, he waited a beat and gathered his breath and whispered, "I would have."

Of course he knew. He had poured every ounce of his spirit into his work on *Beauty and the Beast* and he trusted his spirit like no other.

The four of us left and rode the elevator to the hospital lobby. No one spoke. Howard died a few weeks later.

In early October and weeks before *Beauty* was finished, the New York Film Festival invited us to screen an unfinished version of the film to an opening night audience at Lincoln Center.

If you have ever seen an unfinished clip of animation you know that it looks a bit like a coloring book before the colors are added. The uncolored and colored bits bounce back and forth and the result is really distracting and not particularly pretty.

So with sweaty palms I boarded a jet with the directors and flew to New York for the festival. After showering, dressing, and reciting the Twenty-third Psalm a few times, we took a car from our hotel to Lincoln Center. On the way we didn't say much. We just let the flop sweat trickle down our foreheads. As the car pulled up in front of Avery Fisher Hall, we noticed a teeming crowd of people. I don't know what I expected, but people had actually showed up to see the film. Inside, we ran into some friends and were introduced to reporters. A film crew from *20/20* was there too. They had been following us around for weeks doing a story on the making of the film. As showtime neared, we were hustled to a greenroom and then again to the backstage wings in preparation for some opening remarks. It all felt vaguely like a scene from *Spinal Tap*.

As we walked out onstage to introduce ourselves, the packed house fell silent. We made the usual opening disclaimers and told them that what they were about to see was very rough and a work in progress. That *Beauty and the Beast* is indeed a tale as old as time—a story that has appeared around the world in countless versions like *Cyrano*, *Phantom of the Opera*, and *The Jim and Tammy Faye Bakker Story*.

With that, the lights dimmed and the film rolled. Each song was greeted with a hearty ovation and each joke played like a million bucks. I was stunned by the reaction. Kirk and Gary and I were so close to the film—so engrossed in the process of finishing it on time—that we had lost track of the notion that someday an audience would sit down in a darkened theater and enjoy it. That someday was today.

We had taken our seats in an opera box at the side of the theater where the filmmakers of past festivals sit while the audience takes in the show. When the final note sounded, the audience erupted. We stood in our box like stunned mule deer and waved to the audience as they proceeded to come unglued for about ten minutes. I'll always remember that moment. Standing there in an opera box in front of a cheering crowd is about as close as I'll come to feeling like Eva Perón.

Who'd have thought it? Howard would have, and we missed him very much that night. When the film was released that November it bore this dedication:

> To our friend, Howard, who gave a mermaid her voice
> and a beast his soul.
> We will be forever grateful.

6

THE

SENSES

Our consciousness is based largely on what we experience with our eyes, nose, hands, ears, and mouth. We use the same senses to bring our creations to life and communicate our creative impulses. Until we master mental telepathy or grow another more advanced head, these are the physiological tools we have to work with.

Some ideas spring from a frail and transient spark—an abstract image in your mind's eye. Others hit like a lightning bolt. All ideas follow a path of transformation from an energy bolt in the brain into the real physical, sensual world.

These sparks of creativity will either evaporate in our minds or they will become the focus of conscious thought and desire. We call upon our bodies to help physicalize our thoughts into tangible things. As children, our first instinct is to try to communicate through movement. A smile or frown tells so much. Think about a child's face—the scrunched up nose or the wide-eyed look of delight are just as clearly communicative as words could ever be. Children then try to communicate by visual means like drawing, painting, building with blocks, or playing with toys. They make no distinction between work and play, or art and nonart. Their ears are full of sound, their eyes and nose are bombarded with raw color and new scents. Their little hands reach out to feel the textures of life and everything goes into the mouth for taste testing. For a child, life is extremely sensual.

We still live as adults in an equally sensual world and so we value tactile experiences. An idea is just a fleeting impulse of electricity, but an idea that has a physical manifestation is compelling and invites us to explore it with our senses. Somehow the human spirit responds more deeply to that which can be touched and seen and heard and smelled and tasted. Abstract thoughts lack real power until they can be somehow physicalized into a creation that occupies space in the universe.

Writers and musicians use the letters of the alphabet or notes on a page to physicalize their thoughts. It's a sort of code that sits there on the printed page waiting and hoping that you the reader will someday pick up the page, read the code, and use the symbols of alphabet and notation to recapture the thoughts and ideas of the creator. In this way the creator needs *you* to make his or her creation manifest and real.

It's hard for most of us to understand subatomic particles or theories of relativity because they are ideas that are not readily visualized, nor can they be simply experienced. It's easy for us to understand gravity because we feel it every day. It's almost impossible for us to comprehend the notion of space and time bending at the edge of a black hole because it eludes our sensual grasp.

Not only do we struggle with the duality of the dreamer and the doer brain but we also struggle with the duality of intellectual thought versus physical experience. The most successful creative people can justify these two selves into one. They are able to take the quicksilver of fleeting thoughts and capture them like lightning in a jar, then somehow turn this lightning into a physical entity with mass, volume, and character. Creation, then, is the physicalization of abstract thought into a tangible, understandable form.

Birth

Imagine how a newborn baby feels. One day it's in a warm dark comfortable womb, the next it's thrust into the cold and noisy world of pacifiers, applesauce, and the Teletubbies. Its senses are bombarded. Everything is new.

You were once that baby. Somewhere in the back of your brain you know what it feels like to be a newborn when everything was full of wonder. Every face, every storybook, every lullaby was a new experience. Babies make mental connections at alarming rates while trying to figure out this new world they live in. At birth, a baby's brain contains roughly as many nerve cells as there are stars in the Milky Way. The first five years of life are full of an unimaginable capacity to learn. A child's brain makes endless connections of logical patterns and at the same time begins to eliminate connections and patterns that are never used. This growth and pruning process leaves behind a teenager whose shaved head and snappy nose ring reflect a set of emotions and patterns of thought that are completely unique.

Baylor College of Medicine researchers have found that babies who are seldom touched or who rarely play can develop brains that are 20 percent to 30 percent smaller than normal. Play and stimulation, especially during the early years of life, form the foundation of visual, emotional, verbal, and physical traits of the young person and eventually the adult.

Babies grow into adults, and as adults we find a job, a spouse, and a home and settle down into a predictable and pleasant routine. We break the routine by vacationing for a few weeks every year when we figure we should stretch our senses with a visit to places like the Grand Canyon, New York City, or Orlando's Gatorland, "Home of the Famous Gator Jumparoo!" (I'd like to take a moment to highly recommend the Jumparoo, since it's one of the only places on earth where you can watch an alligator stalk through the water with only its eyes and nose exposed and then leap seven or eight feet out of the water and bag an entire chicken in one gulp. As the employees of Gatorland will tell you, "This is not a natural behavior.")

Our senses needn't wait until vacation to come alive. We can search for ways to be reborn into a world of refreshed senses every day, every instant. To open our senses requires a renewed commitment to awareness of the world and a new commitment to our wellness.

Awareness needs time. Time to spend with your spouse or child. Time to stop and really look at yourself and your environment. I did this one year and realized that my big problem was boxes. My office, my home, my garage, and even my car were always full of boxes. I don't even know what was in most of them but it wasn't useful stuff like books or ski clothes. Most of my boxes contain an assortment of unrelated items that you would never see together under normal circumstances: a baseball glove; a Mounds bar; a battery charger for a long-lost appliance; a map of Provo, Utah; three sticks of beef jerky; a hand towel; a brochure called *Sinus Congestion and You*; a fruit-cake circa 1978; a John Tesh cassette; a shower cap from the Residence Inn; and a jar containing nails, buttons, paper clips, and dice. I thought of burying this box in my backyard as a time capsule. People would dig it up in a hundred years and enjoy the fruitcake as they marveled at my primitive means. But instead I vowed to spend the new year eliminating the cursed corrugated demons from my life.

Along with cleaning out our senses, I like what many of the innovative doctors and nutritionists are starting to say about wellness. They are beginning to look at health as a mental, physical, and spiritual condition and along with prescribing good food and adequate sleep, they are also beginning to prescribe time for meditation and prayer, time for music and fresh flowers in your home, fewer cups of coffee and *Action News* telecasts and more steam baths, walks, and garlic. All of this leads to a renewed and receptive sense of being alive.

A sensual appreciation of life is what allows us to step into the mind of Monet, Proust, and Brahms by seeing, reading, and listening to them describe their feelings in paint, words, and melody. These great artists were once living souls who wore pants and had headaches and bad hair days. We can tune into their feelings by tuning into their work. Each created a vivid snapshot of what life was for them—an emotional record of their existence. Life is lived heartbeat to heartbeat. What we experience in each heartbeat is what drives our creative spirit. When we open sensually to our environment and immerse ourselves in life's natural wonders of birth, death, and renewal, we begin to learn about creation from a very intuitive and natural place. Just as our cave-dwelling ancestors didn't have to be taught how to paint on their cave walls we needn't turn always to books and teachers for instruction in creativity.

When you were a child, you were taught how to do everything: how to read, how to write, how to behave in public, how to fold your socks. In nearly every area of life, we have been taught the right way to do things. So when we begin to create, we think we should know how to go about it. But creating is one thing that we should *not* know how to do. The essence of creation is not knowing, of moving from the unknown and mysterious to the known and revealed.

Seeing

You can see a lot by observing.

—YOGI BERRA

We do a lot of looking but very little seeing. Looking and seeing both start with the same eye, but that's where the similarity ends. Seeing implies a deeper look—more than the cursory glance we give most people, places, and things. If creative beings were meant to interpret their world, then we had better start seeing the world with insightful eyes.

Drawing, painting, and photography require careful see-ing, but so do playing tennis and playing the stock market.

Many have ears but few hear. Many have eyes but few see, and even fewer see the world in much more than just a utilitarian way. We are called to not only observe the world we live in but to create a point of view of that world for the consideration of others. The audience may laud or hate the view but it is our job as a link in the evolutionary chain to create a view so that others can see. Just as we stand on the shoulders of our ancestors, our descendants will turn to us for a perspective on life.

We do it all the time with our children. We stop to explain, we draw with them, we bend down and show them how to shoot a free throw. Then when we have to share our vision of the world with other adults we stop short. Our inner editor says, "Why would anyone want to see my view, they have their own view." But that's where we are wrong. No person, and particularly no creative per-son, is an island. We all feed off other points of view and other perspectives. Without looking at the world from the teacher's viewpoint or the preacher's viewpoint or the painter's viewpoint, we wouldn't have a particularly broad-based opinion of life.

Seeing constitutes not only seeing with your own eyes and interpreting what you have seen for others, but also seeing what others have interpreted for you.

In a way, light is like sound. If no one is there to hear it, it doesn't make a sound. And so if no one is there to see, the light is in some sense meaningless. It is *your* eye that gives it meaning and a sense of place and value. So in that way, nothing can be seen in a truly objective way. When you study an object with your eyes, you will be forever changed by it and it by you.

Listening

So many works of creation are for a general audience. This book would be so much more interesting if it were written specifically for you. If I knew you better and I could speak to you through these words, I could tell you about parts of my life and then listen as you would tell me about yours. I could tell you that you look very nice right now but you still have a little bit of chocolate chip cookie left on your cheek from the last chapter. A book, like a play or a film, speaks to a very large, diverse audience.

By doing test screenings of movies, filmmakers can actually listen to what the audience has to say in response to the work. It's a unique feature of the arts.

There is a man in Hollywood whom we'll call Günner Bergenvjorn. Günner is a pollster who recruits and surveys test audiences for movies. He is either the most-beloved or most-hated man in Hollywood, depending upon how your film is testing with the audience. Market research for a motion picture is a cruel process.

When a film is almost completed, we take it to an out-of-town theater and Günner recruits about 500 people from a shopping mall to come and see our unfinished movie. The film is screened and then the audience is asked to fill out a questionnaire about their feelings. Was it too long, boring, confusing? What did you like about the characters? The music? Would you recommend this film to your friends?

After a typical preview screening, the directors and I usually huddle with a few executives at a local restaurant, drinking beer and eating from the appetizer menu of deep-fried cheese logs and buffalo chicken wings with blue

cheese dressing (something about the shock of all this cho-
lesterol in the system makes the process of previewing
much more enjoyable). Sometime after the nachos and before the potato skins, Günner bursts in with the results.
We are told that 87 percent of the audience would recommend this film; 45 percent liked the opening song best;
57 percent had families and children with them. Every
demographic was nailed down and every reaction recorded.

And what you find after this grueling process is that
most of the movie works, but some parts were unclear and
need work. You also learn that some jokes didn't fire off
like you thought, and that you will get severe heartburn if
you eat deep-fried cheese logs with blue cheese dressing
at eleven o'clock at night. The scrutiny of Günner and his
audiences will force you to look hard at the work and
make some changes based on what the audience felt. But
far and away the most common change made after a preview is one that a director or executive suggests just based
on instinct.

On *The Lion King*, we previewed the film to very fa-
vorable reviews, but the directors had a very strong feeling
about a moment in the film after Mufasa's ghost had appeared to Simba. The moment ended with Simba sitting
silently on a hillside in awe at what had just happened
and we faded to black. We were really missing a moment
where someone "framed" for us, as the audience, the
events that had just happened. At the same time Michael
Eisner felt like the audience loved Rafiki and sensed that
we needed more of him in the film.

The directors, writers, and story people went back to
the drawing board the next day and wrote a scene with
Rafiki and Simba. Simba says he's worried about his past

and then Rafiki steps up and thumps Simba on the head with his stick.

"Hey, what was that for?" cries Simba. Rafiki responds, "It doesn't matter, it's in the past."

In almost riddlelike fashion, Rafiki outlines a crucial theme of the movie: You have to put your past behind you. We previewed the movie three weeks later with the new scene included—a scene that the audience hadn't asked for but that we felt they missed—and the results were great. Not only did the new scene give context to the moment but it did it with a smile.

We listened to Günner's audience. The key, however, was not giving the audience what they literally wanted, but giving them a clearer vision of what the filmmakers were trying to say. Filmmaking, like writing or painting, is a way of interpreting the world through the eyes of a particular artist. It's not about studying market surveys or trends in pop culture. For *The Lion King*, we could never have imagined that anyone aside from our mothers would want to see a movie about a lion cub who gets framed for murder and takes refuge with a flatulent warthog and a showtune-belting meerkat. But they did.

And finally, listening demands that we not jump into the conversation prematurely with our own conclusions. I came home from work one day to my little girl. I had been working a lot of extra hours and had a healthy amount of paternal guilt for not being with her enough, so I scooped her up when I came in the door and gave her a big daddy hug.

"I missed you today, sweetie," I said and then she looked up at me and said, "Daddy," tears welled up in her eyes, "my little heart is broken."

My stomach sank. I had been away too long and all

my guilt was welling up inside. "I'm sorry honey, what's the matter?"

"My little heart broke today."

"Oh, I'm so sorry, how come?"

She started to cry a little and I gave her a hug as she reached into her pocket for something. It was her little heart-shaped necklace.

"My little heart . . . I sat on it and it broke."

What people are saying is not always what you think they are saying. Listen carefully.

Smell

I have very little to say about smell. Some things smell great and other things smell stinky. And it's not the same for everyone. One person's great is another person's stinky, and vice versa. I'm intrigued by the future of odors. It's not enough to enjoy life's naturally occurring odors like a freshly mowed lawn or bread fresh from the oven. Now we can have pleasing odors on demand. It happened to me at the car wash the other day. I drove up and asked for a wash and a hot carnuba wax and the gentleman with the clipboard asked me, "And what scent would you like today?"

If memory serves me right, that was the first time in r. y life that anyone asked me that question. I guess the idea of selecting a scent for your body in the form of a cologne or perfume isn't that unusual, so why not pick a scent for my car?

"What do ya have?" I asked.

"Well, we have lemon, cherry, strawberry, pine, vanilla, and new car."

I wasn't sure that I wanted to smell like timber all week and the rest sounded more like Kool-Aid flavors than car scents. New car was the only choice. I love the smell of new car. Every new car that my dad bought smelled that way. Sometimes in the evening after dinner we would go out to the garage and just sit in the car so we could smell that smell.

"New car," I said.

The car was then whisked away from me, washed, dried, and rubbed with a hot carnuba, which I presumed was a small mammal from Central America. When all was done, I tipped the attendant and hopped in the driver's seat poised for a nostril full of memories. I exhaled deeply to clear as much room as possible in my waiting lungs and I drove off. Then as I started my big inhale, my eyes widened in confusion. This wasn't the smell of new car. Not at all. I spun around and roared back to the attendant.

"This smell, it's not new car—what is it?"

He stuck his head in. "Oh yep, that's new car all right."

I got the guy with the clipboard to come over and try it with the same results, and then I got the vacuum guy, the manager, the lady in the gift shop, and the buff-and-detail guy to all come over until about sixty people were hovering around and smelling my car.

The vacuum guy was most poetic, sounding more like a sommelier discussing a fine wine: "It's not new car, but it has overtones of berries and lemon with a finish of leather."

"Oh, no, no, no," said the manager. "It *is* new car but it's mixed with the smell of the hot carnuba." Well, I don't know about you but if this was true I didn't want to drive around smelling like a hot Central-American mammal for the next six weeks. I started wondering if the cherry and the pine smelled that bad, too. They'd have a lot less customer dissatisfaction if they'd just ask you up front if you wanted the dead squirrel, messy pants, bad gouda, or hot Central-American mammal. You'd say no, they'd wash your car, and everyone would go home happy.

Finally, after much group sniffing and discussion, the investigation proved conclusively that the attendant definitely gave me the new-car scent and the fact that it smelled more like the new cars smelled in Costa Rica instead of America was moot. It was to be my odor for weeks to come.

I wanted so desperately to relive those nights from my childhood when after dinner we went out to take a whiff of the new Rambler, but it wasn't to be. Some sense memories just can't be recreated.

Feeling

Feeling doesn't come just from your hands. It's a full body experience. Many years ago I actually looked forward to going to the family dentist because it was a sensory smorgasbord. First of all, upon arrival, we would sit in a waiting room that was festooned with magazines. As my mom would flip through the latest *Life* or *Time*, I would gravitate to a children's magazine called *Highlights*. It was the kind of magazine that was full of puzzles and riddles: "Why was the cookie sad? His mother was a wafer a long time."

Occasionally they would have a short story like "Adventure on the Mountain," which usually contained a little drama about freeing a stuck beaver or something. I loved *Highlights* anyway because it was filled with drawings of all kinds. There were the "Goofus and Gallant" stories about two brothers. One would study hard, help out at home, and light the candles in church while the other was busy hiding dog poop in the neighbor's newspaper. I was strangely drawn to these morality tales.

Then there was the find-the-object section where you looked at a drawing of, say, a peaceful beach scene, and had to locate the hidden objects like fishhooks in the surf and umbrellas in the clouds.

I loved the riddles and would torment my mother with them.

"Why did the bicycle lean against the fence?"

"I don't know."

"You have to guess."

"Because no one was riding it?"

"No, because it was too tired . . . get it?! Two tired . . . two tires!"

This usually elicited smiles from the other adult patients because the punchlines were funnier than the root canals that they were awaiting.

Every few minutes, the door would open and the dental assistant, Miss Welch, who looked to my developing eyes to be Raquel Welch's pretty younger sister, would open the door and chirp out a name. The chosen one would turn ashen and rise slowly to follow Miss Welch into the bowels of the office. About an hour went by when Miss Welch opened the door and called "Mr. Hahn?" I was relieved that she was calling for my father, but my mom reminded me that Dad wasn't with us and that I was Mr. Hahn. I followed Miss Welch, who led me into the dentist's office.

I walked past the other rooms with their doors shut. I could hear the faint and unusual noises of drill bits whirring and saliva being sucked through a tube at high rates of speed. I was ushered into the examination room where my visit began with a staggering series of mouth X-rays. Miss Welch would begin by saying that these were extremely low levels of radiation that would cause absolutely no harm. Then she proceeded to don what appeared to be a lead barbecue apron, goggles and gloves, and point a cone-shaped ray gun at the tip of my nose.

She placed a piece of cardboard in my mouth and said, "Bite down and hold still." Miss Welch disappeared behind a lead screen to press the button. While I waited for my jolt of radiation, I sat frozen with a mouth full of cardboard and glanced around the room at what appeared to be a small machine shop.

Just then the dentist broke in and upon seeing that I was being bombarded with radiation said the comforting words "Oh, *jeez*" while ducking out to avoid being exposed. When Miss Welch was through, she stripped off my lead apron and gave the dentist the all clear sign. He burst in with a hearty round of "good morning, how ya doin' . . . those are just routine X-rays that cause absolutely no harm" and went to work. I sat in a room that was reserved for kids. Amid the machinery were large cutouts of Goofy, Chip 'n Dale, Bugs Bunny, and other cartoon characters who were presumably selected because of their abysmal teeth, as if to say, "If you're not careful there, Donny, you'll end up lookin' like the Goof."

As the dentist worked away, he would tell me what he was doing with his tools, which he had named something like Mr. Mirror and Mr. Pick. This was supposed to make his young patients feel better although I was never quite sure why a child would find comfort having his young gums explored by Mr. anybody. The environment was like nothing I had ever seen on the planet Earth. I stared up at

Goofy while Mr. Pick probed my incisors and Miss Welch hovered nearby and I thought, How would you describe this to someone from another planet?

> So I was shown into this sterile dark room and forced to sit in a chair. A beautiful girl in a lead suit bombarded my body with radiation and then a guy in a white coat came in and shined this impossibly bright light into my eyes while he started investigating my mouth with a metal probe.

I even have this theory that a lot of people get confused as they get older and mistake this childhood experience for an alien abduction. The tabloids are full of stories that read just like this. I loved the dentist office because it was a place where I could feel all the known emotions at one time—fear, love, joy, hate, pain, sorrow, suction—right there in the dentist's chair.

Taste

I eat out every once in a while at one of a few favorite restaurants. I must point out that I haven't completely given myself over to the new cuisine of baby corncobs with duck and pomegranate polenta. Every once in a while I enjoy a meal of comfort food. Food that tastes familiar and like an old friend.

The Smoke House is across from the old Warner Brothers studios in Toluca Lake. It's a place like Sardi's or the Brown Derby that serves not only food but nostalgia. Their waitresses and busboys are warm and friendly and have a combined age of three hundred thousand years. It's a place where Bob Hope came to have lunch with Bing Crosby.

We came here often—once to celebrate my grandpa's eightieth birthday at that table over there by the lobster tank. It's a place where the deep burgundy booths have cradled the bottoms of hungry punters for decades and fulfilled their need for daily bread and conversation. When I have lunch there, I always feel like having a martini and the prime rib. The taste of horseradish gives me the nose-clearing sensation that I had twenty years ago when I had my first "king's cut" over there in booth thirteen. And then there's the garlic bread. Only occasionally does God give man the gift of such perfection. I always thought that if the planet were being destroyed tomorrow and I had to get on a spaceship to leave but was only allowed to take ten things, I'd take Picasso's *Guernica*, a copy of Shakespeare's *Hamlet*, anything by Mozart, a Bible, the Beatles' anthology albums, a print of *Citizen Kane*, the 1967 Volkswagen Beetle, Miss Welch, a change of underwear, and an order of the garlic bread from the Smoke House. With these things one could form a suitable colony on any planet.

With these foods in this setting, taste becomes more than just a sensation of the tongue. I love these foods because I associate them with the added comfort of good times and good company—of dinners long past with my family. The chicken teriyaki reminds me of my sister and the cheesecake was my mom's favorite. I'm sure that when I was a teenager sitting there with my family I didn't have the same feelings. The food was great, but I was more concerned about what I was going to wear to the Helen Reddy concert that night. But now those years of tasting and sampling have given me a menu of things that not only taste good but bring the added comfort of good memories and happy times.

The tongue not only tastes bitter, sweet, salty, and sour, but it also tastes familiarity. There is another definition of the word *taste* that means a predilection, an aesthetic in art, clothes, and conduct. This taste comes from the same kitchen as our taste for food. Our experiences with food and family around the dinner table breed in us a taste for certain flavors and sensations that are special and unique to us. Our taste in art and conduct come from the same process of hunting for sensations that please and eliminating choices that displease.

As much as I love to experience new flavors in life and in food, I have moments when I want to come back to the Smoke House and taste the familiarity of warm garlic bread and burgundy booths. I can see my grandpa opening his presents and laughing over by the lobster tank and imagine myself in booth thirteen tossing back my first prime rib as Bob Watch-Out-for-That-Horseradish Hope and Der Bingle chat nearby.

Of Dreams and Party Nostrils

Our sixth sense—our intuition—comes in many packages. When we intentionally think, our thoughts seem to follow some logical, predictable direction. We think, What will we have for dinner? . . . How about pizza? . . . No, we had that last night . . . meatloaf . . . I feel like something spicy. . . . Maybe Thai or Indian . . . or Scottish . . . that's it! We'll have haggis. Our thoughts move in a pretty orderly fashion that leads to a solution.

But when our attentions are on some mundane task like walking, or snapping beans, our thoughts move on to an instinctive place. Even though we are occupied with some menial task, our brain is able to daydream on its own. It doesn't need any direction or criticism, it just dreams naturally, sometimes darting back and forth between the dreamer and doer, piecing together a very abstract puzzle that might confound us during more conscious, directed thought.

From this playful side of the brain comes leisurely solutions and jolts of brilliant possibilities that drop into our conscious minds like a voice from heaven. The task, then, is to carve out some time to let yourself daydream. If part of your day is filled up with routine tasks like laundry or lawn mowing, great. It's that kind of repetitive task that can occupy your body while your mind has time to think.

When you feel like your creative well has run dry, it doesn't help to sit there and stare at a blank canvas all day. It can be just as productive to get up and wax your legs (or car, depending upon your preference). Hit a tennis ball hard for an hour or take a long walk. Do some gardening or bake a cake. Swim, take a drive, clean the house, make some headcheese—just pick a boring repetitive task (life is full of them) and dive in. And don't think about it too much, either. Just go ahead and jump into your task and the brain will intuitively go into play mode.

A lot of people keep notepads by their showers, bedsides, or in their cars. There is something about the flow of water or traffic that solicits motion and energy in our thoughts. Some people go to bed with a problem in mind and let their subconscious work while they rest. I did this once and woke up at about 3:00 A.M. with what seemed like a major idea for a new motion picture. I jotted down the idea with eight pithy words and went back into a deep and contented sleep. In the morning I remembered being thrilled with my idea. I couldn't wait to expand on it in the bright light of a new day and I glanced at my notepad to read: *Men fight salvo ants and eat party nostrils.* (This film will not be in production soon.)

My favorite place to daydream is the bathtub. My tub dreams started when I was living in England. I would have really busy days dealing with artists and technical problems and then at the end of the day in London, the calls would start to stream in from Los Angeles where it was only nine in the morning. By the time the entire planet was informed, it was nine at night for me and time to walk home. I lived less than a mile away from our studio. The walks home were time to decompress and sort through the day's thoughts while I picked up some groceries at a corner store run by a surly German woman who looked exactly like the barmaid at Oktoberfest.

At home, I'd check the mail, put out the milk bottles, and turn on the tap to fill the tub. All of my best thoughts seemed to come to me while I took a bath. I lived in a basement flat that had one of those really big English bathtubs that consumes all the hot water produced that day by the NATO allies just to fill it up. When it was full, I'd put BBC-1 on the radio and slip into the water with only my eyes and nose sticking out (like that gator stalking the chicken at the Jumparoo). After soaking in a comfortable place for a while, I'd prop a towel under my head and start daydreaming. Then the ideas would come.

Sometimes I'd think about work. Sometimes try to solve a problem. Most of the time, however, my bathtub thoughts would just drift around from place to place and connect unrelated topics. For example, one night I had just returned back from a concert of classical music.

It was a program of Mozart, Brahms, and Wagner played by a mature symphony orchestra, conducted by a tuxedo-clad, baton-wielding band leader. It wasn't great. The Wagner wasn't bad because it reminded me of those Brunhilda types with tin bras and Viking helmets. The rest of the program was pretty pedestrian. I don't know, maybe it was me, but it seemed like symphony orchestras were in decline. Don't get me wrong, it was a perfectly fine program of music, but all in all it was a bit boring.

How could you spice things up a little? At the same time, I couldn't help thinking that sports franchises are booming. What are they doing right? Stadium construction is at an all-time high and players' salaries have eclipsed the national budget of Burundi. Why aren't symphonies thriving like baseball? They're both entertainment. They both take place with a crowd gathering to watch the players. Why don't they borrow ideas from professional sports to make the experience in the concert hall more enjoyable for the fans and therefore more successful.

The typical symphony program includes several tried-and-true compositions by a handful of composers like Mozart, Beethoven, Wagner, and the like. The typical concert goer has heard the pieces before and knows how they will turn out. The entertainment comes from the exquisite mastery of the music and the ensemble playing of the orchestra. There's really no surprise or shock at the concert unless the conductor's pants were to fall down. The audience experience is one of quiet appreciation (for the concert, not the pants falling down).

A baseball fan might go to see her favorite catcher or batter. A concert goer never goes to see his favorite viola player. I think there should be more stars in the symphony. How? Introduce the players like they do at a ball game or even a boxing match: "Sitting in the fourth chair and playing first viola . . . Manny Mota (*everyone cheers*). On bass

drum and later he'll be playing xylophone . . . Ty Cobb
(*more cheering*), and the starting conductor in the orange
trunks, weighing in at one hundred sixty-five pounds . . .
Esa-Pekka Salonen!" This would add a little more personal
contact between fan and player.

The other problem I find with attending the symphony
is that you always know the outcome. You'd never go to
the baseball game if you knew that the final score would
be 3-0. Even if the players execute their game beautifully,
a game with a predetermined outcome has lost its drama.
And I'd also do away with the program that tells what
they're going to play next. Why do it? Can you imagine
opening a baseball program and finding a list of their
plays: "In the fifth inning, Mr. Piazza will attempt to get
on base by bunting the ball, after which Mr. Scott will hit
a pop foul into the nacho shack on the mezzanine. There
will be a brief intermission in the seventh inning."

I don't think the fans would go for this and I don't see
why concert goers should like this either. Let's sit in the
concert hall and be surprised by the next number. You
heard me, let's be surprised. Maybe they start playing a
violin concerto and end up playing Stravinsky. Maybe if a
conductor's not doing so hot, the manager can come in and
take him out of the concert. Why not? I don't want to see
a struggling pitcher, why should I want to see a struggling
conductor? They could even get into a shouting match and
start kicking dirt on each other. I'd pay money to see a
bassoon player get ejected from the game.

Heck, let's put a couple of orchestras up there and see
if they can outdo each other. Just once, wouldn't you like
to go to a concert with 60,000 screaming fans and listen to
the New York Phil and the Chicago Symphony try to out-
play each other? And would it be so wrong to put luxury

boxes in concert halls so that you could eat hot dogs and drink beer with your business clients?

Of course, all this would start to attract advertisers and television. I can imagine that Nike swoosh on everyone's tuxedo jacket. There would be new shoe endorsement deals, a dance squad, a furry mascot, and probably the equivalent of ESPN that would carry the latest scores and news about trades: "In a major development, Philadelphia just traded away two first violinists to San Antonio in exchange for a flautist, two oboes, and a first-round draft pick. Next week is the All-Star break concert where once again the East will try to overcome the dominance of the West over the past five years. And now back to live coverage of Mahler's Fifth."

As I drained the water from my tub and started to towel off, I was convinced that the philharmonic should merge with major-league baseball. They could celebrate by having a free helmet night for kids ten and under the next time they played Wagner. There might even be an ESPN2 that carried extreme music events like the bagpipe battle of the bands and Bill Clinton playing his sax.

Sure, all of this might breed problems. Musicians might start spitting chaw and grabbing their privates and yes, occasionally you'd have a bench-clearing brawl between opposing orchestras, but in the end, I think classical music events would have more vitality and drama, and we'd be better off for it.

Free-associating in the bathtub may seem pointless and it probably is to a degree, but it does give us some much-needed mental playtime. And the intellectual muscles that we daydream with are the same muscles that we think creatively with. It stands to reason, then, that a certain amount of bathtub thinking will foster a sense of comfort when it comes to brainstorming new ideas with colleagues or thinking blue-sky thoughts at the workplace. Sometimes dreaming has no other specific purpose than to let our spirits fly. I rarely act on my bathtub thoughts. I certainly didn't pick up the phone and call the L.A. Philharmonic with these ideas, but last time I went to a concert I did sort of wish that the peanut guy would come around.

REBIRTH

Man's main task in life is to give birth to himself.

—ERICH FROMM

Picasso said that when he was a child he could draw like the old masters, and it took him the rest of his life to learn to draw like a child. People talk a lot about discovering the inner child—that innocent creative toddler yearning to be free, but no one ever tells you what to do with Junior once you've discovered the little tyke within you.

When experts address the subject of finding the ideal creative spirit, the ultimate creative machine, the best that I can figure out is they are referring to how you felt as a kid. So when you get ready to release your inner child, let's think about what you will be releasing. The average five-year-old is just learning how to read, wears underwear emblazoned with princesses or superheroes, frequently spills things on his or her clothing, and is just starting to learn the really good knock-knock jokes.

This ideal creative spirit spends four hours in kindergarten which seems to be a mixture of drawing, singing, dancing, reading, studying dinosaurs, working with clay, painting, and climbing the monkey bars. The remainder of their time is spent running at top speed, screaming loudly, giggling, crying, being hugged and kissed by adults, bathed by a caretaker, dressed in uniformlike pajamas, and put to bed.

Now let's take a look at the average adult—the adult who is meant to acquire the attitude of the five-year-old. The average adult works eight or nine hours a day, wears white underwear rarely emblazoned with princesses or superheroes (only during the height of mating season), makes grunting sounds when rising from a chair or sofa, spends four hours a day eating or preparing food, spends two hours watching television, and fifteen minutes with their five-year-old.

How on earth are these two seemingly diverse species ever going to get together? Even if one took on the characteristics of a tot, the physical exertion would land you in the hospital and the behavior—running, screaming, giggling, crying, spilling food, missing a tooth—would land you in an institution where you would indeed be bathed by a caretaker, dressed in uniformlike pajamas, and put to bed. How, then, are we truly expected to rediscover the inner child?

When was the last time you made something from clay or picked up a paintbrush and painted something? When was the last time you ran as fast as you could or tried the monkey bars? There is a feeling that we had when we were five years old. It was that feeling that everything was new. Every leaf and dog, every song and book was a new and unique experience. A hot dog was fine cuisine and ice cream was even finer. The Sunday comics were literature, *Mister Rogers' Neighborhood* was theater, and Little League was world-class sports. You were a beginner at everything, but you probably didn't mind. All you wanted to do was learn and move on to the next new thing.

To be a kid again means becoming a beginner again. It's a difficult sacrifice since we've worked our entire life building the experience and knowledge that we've so desperately wanted. But it is far more important to discover that feeling of newness.

As adults we attempt to become new again in many ways. There is the corporate retreat method where we take the humdrum schedule, pressure, and problems of our work-a-day world and move them to a hotel conference room in the mountains or at the beach. Here we are handed an eight-hour schedule of meetings plus roughly four hours of eating or food preparation and two hours of watching television in our room before calling our spouse on the phone for fifteen minutes. The adult pattern is not effectively broken.

A more interesting approach might be four hours of a mixture of drawing, singing, dancing, reading, studying dinosaurs, working with clay, painting, and climbing the monkey bars, followed by a period of running, screaming, giggling, crying, and spilling food. I'm exaggerating a little bit, but not much. To let the adult have a day off would let the child return and with it, the childlike properties of curiosity, questioning, intuition, and emotion.

So in discussing the birth and development of your creative self, I've used these handy terms from the birth and development of a baby:

Make room for baby
Prepare a nursery
Announcing the good news
Keeping a baby book
Care and feeding
Toys and playthings
Postnatal depression
Empty nesters

Make Room for Baby

On your quest to exhume your creative spirit, you will feel silly, you will think it won't work, you will feel dumb, you will revert to comfortable ways, you will say lots of negative things to yourself. There is going to be a constant conversation between the parent in you and the new child in you and the knee-jerk response will be to obey the adult voice.

In American popular culture, we gravitate toward the logical part of the brain and for mostly good reasons. Who'd want a child doing the accounting, or working on the next Space Shuttle launch? These are jobs for logic-minded grown-ups. Logic appreciates neatness and likes life to work in an orderly fashion. It enjoys dividing things into categories which it studies and understands in a rational, unbiased way. Our logical brain knows the world is a much better place if it is carefully and neatly organized.

This logical part of the brain is our editor. It's what makes us wince at sour notes and what warns us when something doesn't conform to our definition of art.

Our abstract brain, on the other hand, is the innovative, childlike numbskull who can look at something that it's never seen before and not try to label or categorize it. It simply takes the world at face value. Our abstract brain often thinks without words. It free-associates with patterns, colors, and disconnected ideas.

The abstract brain doesn't stop and count the cost. It looks into the darkness and sees opportunities and adventures. It wants you to leap out and fly into that darkness to experience a fresh updraft of change and of new thought.

The logical brain stands and carefully considers the opportunities before it. It loves familiarity, conformity, and safety. It likes things that it has seen before, people it has met before, food it has eaten before, and clothes it has worn before. When you gaze upon something new, it will send you more warning signals than the robot in *Lost in Space*.

Modern life in a western culture seems to be lived almost entirely in the logical brain and so in a quest for a more creative life, we need to seek more balance and migrate more closely to our abstract thoughts. When your logical brain shouts, "Run, Will Robinson, run!" one way to balance yourself is with a good helping of quiet, focused thought. You can call it prayer, meditation, centering, realignment, or as they say in the business world, stress management, but the search for balance between the logical and abstract brain can help us journey from a superficial perspective to an insightful perspective, from shallow to deep, from physical to spiritual, from panic to peace.

Prepare a Nursery

New discoveries are like newborn babies. They have no name and they seem a little awkward, but there is something very attractive and compelling about them. There is a kinship we have with new ideas.

A nursery is a room or place equipped for young children. It's a room where they can be raised and nurtured and feel a sense of security when the lights go out and the sandman comes. It's a place where you can crawl under the covers with a flashlight anytime you want. When was the last time you had a room that was equipped for you, just you? If you like to cook, it could be your kitchen where you are surrounded by the security of your favorite pots and spices. Sometimes it's a spare bedroom or a garage where you can go to have time alone to think and create. Every creative spirit needs a home, a safe haven for ideas and creative activity.

It needs to be a place where you can go and shut away the outside world and be alone with your thoughts. Some artists find that a mountain cabin or a hot tub is a great place to create. Some do their best problem solving in the car, others in the shower. Wherever it is that you go, we all need a quiet womb where we can create. Groups of artists who collaborate and work together also need a nurturing environment to work in.

For fifty years, Disney animators occupied the animation building on the main lot of Disney studios in Burbank. The great classics of Disney animation were produced in this building. By the early 1980s, animation talent was in transition and the hallways at the Disney studio were full of talent coming and going. Going were veterans Milt

Kahl, Frank Thomas, Ollie Johnston, Mark Davis, and Ken Anderson. Coming were a ragtag collection of artists mostly from CalArts, who occupied the building's D wing, what one well-known animator had dubbed the rats' nest. Fresh from school, Ron, John, Brad, Jerry, Bill, Henry, John, and Tim.

Hollywood was being redefined by filmmakers like Coppola, Scorsese, Spielberg, and Lucas. They were changing the ways we look at movies and in a sense revitalizing the movie business. There was an opportunity for a similar renaissance in animation, but the conditions weren't right. The facility was beautiful, the craft was exquisitely honed, but the passion and creative risk had disappeared.

The D wing of the animation building had become home to a dirty dozen of young twenty-something animators who were working on less-than-blockbuster titles like *The Fox and the Hound* and the disappointing *Black Cauldron*. These nubile artists were starved for artistic leadership and collaboration that unfortunately didn't exist— the studio had become creatively stagnant by trying to repeat well-worn formulas from the past. The young artists didn't have a fertile playing field for their creative aspirations.

A decade later, when we were making films like *Beauty and the Beast, Aladdin*, and *The Lion King*, we were housed in the most drab, utilitarian warehouses possible. (The artists had been moved off the lot to make way for Disney's expanding live-action business.) In one of the buildings, gnats got into the air-conditioning system and if you sat anywhere under a duct, you received a gentle drizzle of dead gnats all day long. In summer you roasted, in winter you froze, and in rain you brought in buckets to catch the dripping water.

Nonetheless, the environment was never better. The artists plastered the walls with caricatures, daily comics were pasted above the urinals, and the rubber band fights were legendary.

It was less about the building and more about the people whose attitude turned those warehouses into a warm womb for creation. The novice young animators had gone on to be some of the most renowned filmmakers of this generation: Ron Clements and John Musker, who made *The Little Mermaid, Aladdin,* and *Hercules*; Brad Bird, one of the founding fathers of *The Simpsons*; Jerry Rees became a live-action director and animation consultant on films like *Space Jam*; Bill Kroyer directed *FernGully*; Henry Selick directed *Nightmare Before Christmas* and *James and the Giant Peach*; John Lasseter reinvented animation with the computer graphics marvel *Toy Story*, and Tim Burton made films like *Batman, Beetlejuice, Ed Wood,* and *Mars Attacks*. Some made their careers at the studio, some did not, but they all lay dormant in the D wing until a changed environment allowed them to flourish.

Building a studio is not just about assembling talents and placing them in a beautiful facility; it's having the courage to listen to them and let them grow and flourish in their own unimaginably unique ways.

Announcing the Good News

There is an old adage: Leap and the net will appear. Commit to an idea and the resources to create it will become apparent. The safety net of creativity is the kinship you form with your fellow creators. So find a very close friend, leave the house, meet for coffee, or better yet, a huge meal of haggis with Mr. Cozart's sauce on a bed of baby chicory, and then announce your rebirth. You've got to share this vision someday, it might as well be with friends and haggis.

You are facing a form of upheaval in your life and your support network of family and friends can help. You'll need a safety net for yourself, so seek out the people who will be accepting of you, not blind or uncritical, but accepting and encouraging.

I really believe people don't know how to respond to the news that you want a little more creativity in your life. When you're sick they can say, "Take care now," and when you are sad people say, "That's all right," but there is no socially acceptable response to the fact that you want more innovation and creative spirit. I think it's because the term *creativity* is so vague and covers such vast arenas of creative thought from astrophysics to zoology that most people respond with that what-does-this-have-to-do-with-me look.

Before you go around to solicit the support of friends and family, it may help to focus on the areas where creativity speaks to you. While it's not so easy to encourage the person who says, "I want more creativity in my life," it is very easy to encourage the person who wants to paint more often, or wants to start a gourmet cooking class. Once we do some soul-searching and decide what we love in life, we can focus our creative spirit, and with the support of family and friends, we can follow our muse.

Keeping a Baby Book

Writing is a wonderful focusing mechanism for the soul. It's a way to journal your observations and feelings and write about your conquests and failures.

Scientists keep lab notes, artists keep sketchbooks, and cooks jot down culinary successes and failures. We need a record of the findings, impressions, ideas, events, and feelings of everyday life. We may not remember that nutmeg made the sauce work but we will remember that we wrote it down.

There is a cleansing effect to writing, too. The act of expressing ourselves in an unedited way with pen on paper gives us a chance to stop carrying our thoughts around and literally put them down.

If you are more visually oriented, don't feel pressure to exclusively use words in your journal. Many people tear out magazine pictures, cartoons, newspaper headlines, or Internet articles that inspire them. These form a unique journal of your feelings and inspirations.

You can do a daily painting to journal your feelings or a daily poem or song, too, but the important thing is a regular expression of your feelings. It's crucial that your journal be your private enclave for expression. Your journal is not a thing to share or analyze with others; it is a daily way to articulate your moods and feelings for yourself.

Care and Feeding

Take care of your physical self as well as your mental self. It's hard to create on an empty stomach or with an empty soul. Our physical being is literally a sum of the food, water, and air we take in along with the effect of the environment in which we exist. On some days I balance my diet with grains, dairy, produce, and meat and on other days my four essential food groups consist of sugar, caffeine, chocolate, and Advil.

Physically and spiritually, we are what we eat. Our creativity reflects what we feed our intellect. That might suggest that we should only feed our intellect from a select group of basic intellectual "food" groups. But if you think it's hard to eat five servings of vegetables each day, wait till you try feeding your creative spirit with a regular balanced diet.

It's impossible, and moreover you wouldn't want to control your input or live in a vacuum. It's important not to jump to a moral judgment here. You should have strong moral opinions about your life. You should express them. The temptation is to say that we should feed our spirits on a diet of only good, wholesome input of purity and sanity and reason.

Life is more complex than that. The arena of human existence is a panoply of experience. Don't edit your input. It is crucial to your creative spirit to know as much as you can about the range of life: good and evil, black and white, silence and cacophony, sacred and profane, order and chaos, wealth and poverty, feast and famine, day and night. That's not to say we have to all embrace every human lifestyle, but an openness to the range of human expression, every human expression, is important to feed your creative soul. Some parts of life may repulse you and others may enrapture you, but our very openness to the full spectrum of life helps form our opinions and our creative voices. Creativity is no place for elitism. Pablo Picasso socialized with bullfighters, Beatrix Potter socialized with sheep ranchers (she actually was a sheep rancher), Ernest Hemingway socialized with bullfighters. My point is not that two out of three artists should hang out with bullfighters, or that artists need a relationship to livestock, but that these highly creative people sought inspiration from lifestyles that were simple, honest, real, and atypical.

Art and creation is a response. Sometimes art responds to life with beauty, hope, sincerity, and innocence, and at times with greed, lust, corruption, and outrage. If life is made up of an extreme range of emotions and experiences, then creativity will also reflect that extreme range.

Toys and Playthings

There is one thing that we seem to know so well and so instinctively that it rivals breathing and walking upright as one of the signature traits of humanity. We know how to play.

Art is related to play. In every way, play and art are related as a simple and essential and very human form of expression. Every child knows how to play, but sometimes we inadvertently teach our children to forget how to play. We discourage kids by being overly critical of their work, or by stopping them in the middle of their creative process to tell them they are doing good or not so good. We make them self-conscious about creating or even laugh when they sing off-key or dance funny or don't draw a house the right way—all those things stop us short when it comes to creating again as adults.

As children are judged and introduced to competition in the arts and myths of talent and skill, they begin to wilt and their playful spirit dies a bit. They begin to feel ashamed of a drawing or a dance. Adults push and interfere with well-meaning but misplaced coaching, and the playful child slowly and sadly learns to stick with safer, more measured skills like math and spelling and history. Reading, writing, and arithmetic have a right and wrong answer. Play does not. Art does not.

Play is so instinctive that we don't have to teach our children how to do it. We come prewired and predisposed to play. Kids may struggle with history or math but you can bet that they know how to play Chinese jump rope and climb the monkey bars. Playfulness is a human trait that is buried deep in our genetic past and as such holds great power in our lives. Adults don't need to be taught how to play, either. We just need to allow ourselves to do it. Grown-ups can play equally as well as kids, only the toys are bigger, faster, and more expensive. As managers learn that play is a welcome cousin of creativity, work environments are becoming more tolerant to play.

It's certainly true that in a place like an animation studio, along with the work, you tend to get a lot of pie fights and funny hand sounds. The spirit inside an animation studio is hard to describe, but one might categorize it as a chaotic creative environment. Most of the nondrawing activities center around drinking coffee and shooting rubber bands at your colleagues. Every once in a while someone brings in something cool like a paintball gun or a mummified cat skeleton. One of the animators celebrated his breaks by leaping up onto a desk and singing lengthy Italian recitatives. He didn't speak Italian but that never stopped him from getting a big ovation and a shower of rubber bands. Another animator kept a full-size standard poodle in his office. It was *the* place to visit if you needed a quick tongue bath.

One story person decided to save his spit in a glass jar for two weeks, which he did, proudly displaying it complete with a label—KELLY'S SPIT—on a shelf behind his desk. One day he came in early and quietly emptied the jar, washed it out, filled it with water, and put it back on the shelf before anyone had come to work. At coffee break time he got up and announced, "Hey, what would you give me if I drank my spit?" After wagers were set, he drank his "spit" for a handsome profit. We all gagged for days.

There was Pirate Day when the animators dressed like pirates and raided the legal and accounting staff and there was the day that someone brought in their slingshot. It wasn't just your regular Dennis the Menace variety but a huge slingshot that took three people to operate. Two people held the ends of what looked like a massive rubber band and a third would stand in the middle and pull the sling back into firing position. You would then insert nearly any desired object, like a pug dog . . . er, sorry—I meant to say, like a small plush toy dog, and with a flick of the wrist, the object would go airborne really, really, really far out there and land somewhere near New Guinea. We started in the parking lot by firing water balloons into the street. We graduated to air-worthy fast food—Twinkies, Ding-Dongs, and HoHos. It's nearly impossible to use mere words to describe the feeling of power you get when you can lob your Twinkie two hundred feet in any direction. It is very satisfying. (As an interesting sidebar, The Walt Disney Company does not normally allow people to loft Ding-Dongs from its premises during work hours, but using the proven adage "It's better to beg forgiveness than to ask permission," we continued.)

Once the animators had mastered the outdoor event, they went inside for the more challenging pastime of Indoor Giant Slingshot (soon to be an Olympic medal sport).

The task was to shoot a donut or similar breakfast food across the studio—about one hundred fifty feet with a slight dogleg to the right—and try to hit some meaningful target, such as a small Styrofoam cup full of steaming coffee.

Frosted donuts seemed to work better than glazed and the day-old variety were the most desirable because of their firmness and superior aerodynamic qualities. One by one, the contestants would take turns loading up the giant sling with their buttermilks, long johns, and maple bars, and one by one these airborne baked goods would catapult across the studio and over the heads of cowering new employees on their way toward their dunking destination—a steaming hot cup of Folger's. Each attempt was greeted with the cheers and moans of onlookers who would then politely applaud the effort as though they were watching Lee Trevino sink a birdie at Augusta.

After each attempt, the judges carefully measured the distance from the cup of coffee to the donut and disqualified only one eager contestant who tried to catapult his meatloaf sandwich toward the target. Everyone clearly saw this as a rules violation (as one might expect, flying meatloaf sandwiches obviously belong in the afternoon hurling event).

The winner was an onion bagel with cream cheese that came within a breathtaking six inches of the coffee. An eclair from another contestant came as close but, without the benefit of the frictional properties of cream cheese, it skidded past the target and into a hapless secretary, to the concerted disappointment of the gallery.

Later that year there was some loose and irresponsible talk about buying a catapult. Somebody had seen a television show on these guys in the Midwest who built one so big it could launch a holstein, but we thought better of it.

Postnatal Depression

The brilliant afterglow of launching your creative ship will crash and burn someday if you're not careful. Once you've opened your heart and mind to a more creative life, you will have a day when you will want to chuck it all and return to the safety of the anonymous worker bee world. Here we take a lesson from ancient books on the art of warfare. When the assault on your spirit seems insurmountable, dig in and wait for it to pass. Or another approach made popular in my house—buy chocolate, and wait for it to pass. Then join the battle once more.

Our lives are very goal-oriented. Just as the sporting world rewards the team with the most points at the end of the game, business and commerce rewards great achievements. There is one small fatal flaw buried in the goal-oriented culture.

As we focus solely on the goal, we miss a great deal of life along the way. When the goal is so important that we miss the joy of the process, then the goal-oriented strategy is unfulfilling at best.

The process is the thing. It's the process that is full of striving and yearnings, the end product is in its simplest form merely an artifact of the process. That's not to say that this artifact need not have great value. A movie is the end product of years of process—all creative, be it acting, directing, writing, or cinematography. The artifact of that process is a film that captures the expression and experience of the filmmakers and can also be sold for money.

If the process is the gem, then you might ask, Does the end product need to have a value at all? If an artist paints a painting and doesn't show it to anyone, is it a waste of time or does it have value? The answer is that it has great value and is a very important work of art because this hypothetical artist did show it to someone . . . himself. The process of expressing our feelings on a canvas or in film or poetry is a process of emergence. Our thoughts and feelings emerge in a way that is often unexpected. At times those feelings might be absurd, or childlike, or something that you might consider to be junk, and at other times it can be inspired. We should never be forced or compelled to show our work involuntarily.

What if you really enjoyed writing poetry. It gave you an outlet for your feelings like no other. It gave you quiet time to express some very raw inner thoughts that perhaps you might never express in conversation. Your poems might be sweet and reflective on one day and full of dark inner musings the next. The act of putting these feelings on paper is a wonder-filled purging process—a process that need not be shared with others to be valid. Be content to create for yourself and exhibit only when you find some sort of emotion in your work that you want to share with a viewer.

Empty Nesters

Of all the surprises that the creative process has to yield, this one is the biggest. Sometimes we fear completion. If creation brings with it the pain of inertia and chaos, then one day we should expect to feel the joy of a vigorous creative success upon the completion of our goals. But sadly, our closets are filled with half-written novels, or business plans that never saw action. We face a final haunting fear in our quest for creation and that is the fear of completion.

Completion has consequences. After the joy and celebration has faded, completion means we will have to endure the opinions of our friends and family. We'll be open to criticism and failure. We'll have to wake up from our dreams and return to reality. We may hesitate before we decide to create again because it was too painful the first time around. We may even have grown attached to the process of creating and fallen in love with the team of people we are working with. Completion means feeling loss and emptiness and the fear that our beloved collaborators will be blown to the wind.

Implicit in the act of creation is the act of completion. Projects are like skyrockets that launch into the darkness and flare out in a blaze of glory. We can try to deflect the feelings of loss that we sometimes feel when we complete a big project. We might vow to return to the formula of prior successes or keep the creative team intact for the next project. But the components of a project and the people that put it together will never quite be the same again. The audience and the marketplace will not be the same, either.

Completion of one project is a crossroads that can catapult us into new and different projects and the opportunity to stretch our creative muscles in other directions.

Here is where the conflict between art and commerce is most apparent. The typical artist (be he or she an actor, cook, or poet) may create something that is highly commercial and popular. The businessperson says, "Keep doing what you're doing and I'll keep selling it." But the artist says, "I've done that and I'm ready to move on and try something new."

"Something new," the businessperson says, "but the audience likes what you do now." And there's the rub. Do we stick to the comfort of repeating past successes and risk stagnation, or do we branch out and risk humiliation and failure?

Those decisions at the crossroads of life are part of every creative journey. Everything about creativity is more a journey than a destination. The journey is full of long stretches of road punctuated with tricky intersections, potholes, bad weather, and small side streets that are full of surprises and discoveries. You may have borrowed a good map from someone else but you'll likely find out that the route has changed.

We like the feeling of home and the routine and predictable comfort, but we also like to play and run naked down the highway of life every once in a while because more than anything, it proves to us that we are alive.

EPILOGUE

What a wonderful life I've had! I only wish I'd realized it sooner.

—COLETTE

Years have passed since the belligerent young man in the back of the auditorium voiced his concern about social injustice in Grover's Corners and times have changed. Life goes by so fast, we hardly realize it. My friend Toad married that female trombone player from the marching band. He became a professor of quantum physics at M.I.T. Miss Welch married some guy named Bjorn Gustafsen and moved to Orlando where she forsook her career in dentistry and got a job on the Orlando Magic's dance squad.

Mr. Cozart passed away years ago but on long summer days when the grill is hot and the steaks are thick, he lives on.

And someplace right now on the planet Earth, a group of high school students are staging *Our Town* by Thornton Wilder. And when they are deep into the third act, they'll find with some sadness that Mr. Webb's daughter Emily has just died in childbirth. Before she exits, she asks the stage manager if she can revisit just one day from her past . . . her twelfth birthday. He agrees. Slowly a distant reflection of her past materializes once again into perfect focus.

There they are, her mother and father, their faces young and beautiful again. She sees her little friends all gathered for a party with their parents standing proudly behind them—friends she hasn't seen or thought about in years. She watches with bittersweet wonder the simple and precious acts of this seemingly normal day from her past and speaks softly to the stage manager:

> EMILY: I can't go on. It goes so fast. We don't have time to look at one another. I didn't realize. So all that was going on and we never noticed . . . clocks ticking . . . and Mama's sunflowers. And food and coffee. And new-ironed dresses and hot baths . . . and sleeping and waking up.
> Do any human beings ever realize life while they live it?—every every minute?
> STAGE MANAGER: No. The saints and poets, maybe—they do some.

Now it's late on Sunday and I'm ready to leave the hardware store and head for home. Somehow when I leave Virgil's, and step back outside the safety of the automatic doors, I feel a little anxious. Creativity in the real world seems overwhelming. Maybe it's because the nuts and bolts of real life are less clearly labeled and there's no Bob or Randy to tell me what to do. The ingredients of life don't always come in a small brown paper bag with the receipt stapled on top.

Who can help me? What if I fall? When can I find the time? Where do my dreams fit in a crowded world? How can I lift my head above the awesome daily tasks of life? Why art, why storytelling, why look with new eyes? Why strive for the impossible, why be creative, why do all this? We'd willingly search everywhere for the secrets of creativity like Voltaire's Candide, who traveled the world over, experiencing gruesome adventures, seeking the best of all worlds, only to end up at home on a little farm, where he reminds himself with quiet regularity, "We must cultivate our own garden." In the end, there is no magic formula for creativity out there. It is all within you.

All this searching for creative achievement may seem like a lonely and at times meaningless pursuit on the fringes of society, but it is not. The creative forces at play within us are the essence of our humanity, and there is something truly heroic about it—this heroism of the seeking mind. This willingness to leap into the void, to illuminate the darkness, to remove the blinders from our eyes and from the eyes of our fellow man. It is this heroism of the creator that drives the evolution of the human species and gives validity and meaning to our life's journey. And so all the pain, the insecurity, the buffeting, and the doubt seem justified in the knowledge that we can ultimately soar above the confines of our anxieties and experience something bigger than ourselves. We can offer up our very personal gift to the human project, and in doing so come closer to Aristotle's happiness than ever before.